THE

T

LINCOLN AND AFTER

DICK TAVERNE

THE FUTURE OF THE LEFT

Lincoln and After

JONATHAN CAPE
THIRTY BEDFORD SQUARE LONDON

FIRST PUBLISHED 1974

JONATHAN CAPE LTD, 30 BEDFORD SQUARE, LONDON WC1

ISBN HARDBACK 0 224 00950 8
PAPERBACK 0 224 00961 3

TO MY FRIENDS IN LINCOLN

PRINTED IN GREAT BRITAIN
BY EBENEZER BAYLIS & SON LTD
THE TRINITY PRESS, WORCESTER AND LONDON
BOUND BY G & J KITCAT LTD, LONDON

CONTENTS

INTRODUCTION

This book is inevitably in part a personal story. My political career has involved me to an unusual extent in the conflicts between the different groups that make up the Labour Party. I hope this experience has given me a clearer appreciation of the causes of the Party's present malaise, although many of my former colleagues may well feel that it has made me unduly pessimistic about the Party's future. Few people's views are unaffected by their own circumstances.

The history of my troubles with the Lincoln Labour Party may in itself be of some interest to students of politics, as not a great deal has been written about political affairs at the constituency level despite their obvious importance and their influence on the politics of Westminster. However, my main concern is not with the conflicts of the past but with the future of the Left in Britain, by which I mean the future of the radical alternative to the Conservative Party. I believe that the events leading up to the Lincoln by-election on March 1st, 1973, were of more than local or personal significance because the conflicts in Lincoln were to some extent a microcosm of the disputes within the Party as a whole. The attitudes of the dominant group of the Lincoln Party were, in a somewhat extreme but not unrecognizable form, representative of attitudes within the Party whose influence has increased, is increasing and ought in my view to be diminished.

The future shape of radical politics in Britain is inextricably linked with that of the Labour Party. Since 1929 at the latest, the Labour Party has been the effective radical alternative. If the Labour Party flourishes, there is no room for any other radical party. The Liberals found this in 1962. Their revival in the days of Orpington was short-lived because the state of the Labour Party was healthy. Liberals made their gains only against the

Conservatives and then only in those constituencies where would-be Labour voters saw no chance of a Labour victory. Labour's subsequent successes in the 1964 and 1966 elections killed this Liberal revival stone-dead.

But there is no law of history which states that the Labour Party must continue to be the major party of the Left. Its present internal divisions may prove too deep by now. Its constitutional structure may be too rigid and neither appropriate nor adaptable to the needs of contemporary radical policy. It is true that the Party has faced many crises in the past and has survived them after convalescence periods of varying duration. But recovery has coincided with control of the Party by realists who had something relevant as well as radical to say about contemporary society. The danger now is of domination by those who are incapable of formulating policies which will either prove workable or win votes. In these circumstances, the Labour Party is only likely to win power if there is a total collapse of Conservative Government. Yet if the only hope for the Party depends on a near national disaster, a realignment of the Left in Britain would become more than a possibility; it would be a necessity.

Throughout this book I have found it impossible to avoid the rather unsatisfactory terminology of 'Left' and 'Right'. They are hardly precise adjectives. In fact they are very much Humpty-Dumpty words which mean what the user 'intends them to mean, neither more nor less', and I accept the general tenor of Samuel Brittan's arguments that their use can be seriously misleading in a number of contexts.* But like Brittan I have to accept that they are far from meaningless. Political argument is full of descriptive terms with no precise definition, such as 'working-class', 'middle-class', 'reactionary', 'militant', 'socialist' and 'radical', which still have a legitimate place in argument. When it comes to 'Left' and 'Right' anyone in the Labour Party has a rough idea of what is meant by 'a very left-wing

* S. Brittan, *Left or Right: The Bogus Dilemma* (Secker & Warburg, London, 1968), and 'Further Thoughts on Left and Right', in *Capitalism and the Permissive Society* (Macmillan, London, 1973).

local party' or 'a very left-wing Labour M.P.'. The local parties concerned, like the Lincoln Party, and the individuals concerned, like Members of Parliament who are members of the Tribune Group, would proudly apply the label to themselves. By contrast, outside the Monday Club relatively few people in the three main British political parties boast of being right-wing and hardly any will describe themselves as reactionary. Certainly within the Labour Party 'right-wing' is generally a term of abuse used by 'left-wingers'.

I have tried to confine the use of the term 'Left' to the broad group which regards itself as being on the left of the Conservative Party. When describing those who regard themselves as part of the Left within the Labour Party I have used the phrase 'left-wing'. This may seem an appropriate distinction to older football fans who remember the pre-Ramsey days when wingers were still in vogue, and the left wing operated on the far left side of the field. Mostly I have preferred to describe those whom the 'left-wingers' call 'right-wingers' as 'social democrats'.

Finally, a warning. In the first part of my book, which describes my clashes with the Lincoln Party, I have tried to be fair, to tell the truth and nothing but the truth, and to see the other point of view. But it is an almost superhuman task to do full justice to one's political opponents and I do not pretend that I have. Not everybody can emulate Thucydides, who was able to record his own defeat by Brasidas so dispassionately that one might not suspect the connection between the unsuccessful general and the historian of the same name. I present my own side of the story and it is bound to have flaws.

PART I: LINCOLN

1

BACKGROUND

A chronicle of disputes within the Labour Party should start with a brief picture of the opposing factions. Over the years the areas of dispute have varied and as they varied some of the contestants have changed sides. But by and large, after making all necessary reservations about the dangers of oversimplifying, within the coalition that makes up the Labour Party there are at least two separate groups whose political philosophy conflicts on important points and each of which has sought to dominate the Party. Sometimes one side won a clear-cut advantage. More often than not a truce was declared with an all-purpose formula that meant all things to all men. But so far, neither side has achieved more than a temporary or limited success—the opposition regroups to contest the field again and again until perhaps some day one of the two sides feels that the coalition is not really worth preserving.

One of these groups consists of the 'social democrats', those who were known in the early 1960s as the Gaitskellites and today as the Jenkinsites, although one should add that some social democrats would not necessarily describe themselves as Jenkinsites.

At the end of the 1950s, when my own active involvement in politics began, the chief philosopher of the social democrats was Anthony Crosland whose book *The Future of Socialism* set out the main social democratic case. Social democrats accept the mixed economy. They believe in the goal of a greater economic and social equality, better social and economic security, and an emphasis on community values which is incompatible with leaving society to the free play of the market forces. They do not regard the public ownership of industry as vital to the achievement of their social aims. In striving for social equality they seek to lessen the impact of class distinctions but do not regard the Labour Party as being essentially a class party. They strongly backed the reform of our social laws in the 1960s which some have denounced as introducing the permissive society but which the social democrats would prefer to call the tolerant or civilized society. They are strongly anti-Communist and committed to collective security and the Atlantic Alliance. They were almost universally in favour of British entry into the European Community. They see politics as a practical business in which winning power to put policies into effect is more important than theorizing about the purity of a Socialist faith.

On the left wing of the Party stand those who in the early 1960s were called the Victory for Socialism group and are known today as the Tribune Group. Many of them are Marxists or near-Marxists. To all of them the ark of the covenant is Clause 4 of the Labour Party constitution which pledges the Party to secure the public ownership of the means of production, distribution and exchange. They see politics as primarily about the class struggle in which the Labour Party must be identified with the interests of the working class. Indeed they seek, or feel, a strong emotional identification with 'the workers' even if their own background happens to be middle-class. They sympathize instinctively with every strike because it produces working-class solidarity. The words 'capitalism', 'bosses', 'exploitation of the working man', spring readily to their lips. They believe strongly in the Labour Party constitution as it stands because it enshrines the unions as the dominant partner (provided of course that the union leadership is predominantly left-wing). When it has to be conceded that many wage-earners vote Conservative or show themselves lukewarm about public ownership or other left-wing causes, they explain this aberration in terms of the failings of the milk-and-water Socialists who have refused to arouse militancy amongst the working class.

In general the Tribune Group is less concerned than the social democrats with the preparation of detailed policies; but the economic future they advocate for Britain is one combining a massive extension of public ownership, to ensure a high level of capital investment, with a strict control of imports and strict exchange controls so that a socialist Britain can be isolated from the chill blasts of international capitalism. They are anti-American and anti-Common-Market; mainly neutralist rather than pro-Soviet, although many of them apply rather less stringent standards of criticism to the defects of the Eastern than to those of the Western world.

I do not of course suggest that every member of the Labour Party is either a social democrat or a supporter of the Tribune Group. Most would probably refuse to identify with either, and at different times in the Party's history have given their support to different camps. The centre has on the whole been loyal to the Party leadership, moderate rather than extreme in its instincts and hostile to those who appear to be splitting the Party, whoever they are. Within the Parliamentary Labour Party this centre grouping is sometimes known as the 'soft centre', while it is regarded by others as the personification of sanity and good sense. But as loyalty rather than ideology has been its main characteristic, it has not been one of the main driving forces within the Party.

After the defeat of the Labour Party in the General Election of 1959 the temporary truce which then prevailed between the social democrats and the left-wing was terminated and two major battles were fought. It is worth looking back at both campaigns: they are relevant to the prospects of the Labour Party as a force for radical change today and provided the background to my arrival at Lincoln.

Hugh Gaitskell was at this time the leader of the Labour Party and his style of leadership was a major factor in the internal struggles of the next few years. It is in many ways astonishing what a deep impact Hugh Gaitskell made on the politics of my generation, even though he was never Prime Minister, and indeed not even an exceptionally successful Minister. His period as Chancellor of the Exchequer coincided with an assumption by Britain of an excessive burden of rearmament at the time of the Korean War, a burden which he himself thought necessary. As leader of the Party in opposition he made several serious tactical errors both during the 1959 election campaign and afterwards. And yet today, despite these shortcomings and more than ten years after his death, Hugh Gaitskell remains an inspiration to many who still think of themselves as Gaitskellites. His posthumous influence on his friends and allies, and even on those who did not know him personally but who shared his combination of idealism and realism, has grown rather than diminished with the years. There are very few politicians of whom this will ever be said. All this was the result of the courage and vision he displayed in the years between 1959 and 1962.

Gaitskell decided that if the Labour Party was to be an effective radical party it must shed its doctrinaire commitment to nationalization. He thought it needed a reform similar to the Godesberg programme, whereby the Social Democratic Party of Germany rejected its Marxist roots and launched itself on the road to electoral recovery and eventual power. At the Party Conference held in the autumn of 1959 to analyse the causes of the election defeat, Gaitskell boldly—if rashly—challenged the central tenet of the left wing's faith, Clause 4 of the Party constitution which commits the Party to the principle of public ownership. He said it should be amended in the light of contemporary circumstances.

To the uninitiated the suggestion might have seemed a sensible, almost uncontroversial proposal with obvious electoral advantage. After all, most Labour M.P.s knew very well that a programme of extensive nationalization was a vote-loser. They did not believe in its merits. There had been no suggestion in the 1959 election programme that Labour was planning a wholesale takeover of private industry by the state. Yet the Conservatives could always point to the Party constitution as an indication of its long-term aims. If, in practice, Clause 4 was a dead letter, why encumber the Party with a burden which was electorally disadvantageous?

There can be no doubt today that the existence of Clause 4

has an effect. Members of the Party who do not believe in it can be reminded that they hold a Party card on which Clause 4 is inscribed as the sacred text. They are forced to be on the defensive. When challenged about their attitude to Clause 4 they mutter phrases about final goals subject to questions of timing. They feel embarrassed about denying the true faith to which they are committed by the constitution. They are therefore forced into a false position of pretending to agree with the left wing about strategy, while admitting only to a difference about tactics. It leaves the left wing in the constituencies with a moral advantage in ideological argument, and in left-wing circles arguing ideology is a popular pastime.

I recall a rather significant incident at a meeting I had with the Newcastle University Labour Club some thirteen years after the 1959 conference which in a way illustrated why Gaitskell felt it necessary to reform Clause 4. It happened after my resignation from Parliament but some months before my re-election. Because of the notoriety I had attracted, there was an unusually large number of students present—about seventy-five—when normally meetings of Labour clubs at provincial universities do well to muster more than thirty. I expounded my views on social democracy, including the need to accept a mixed economy and to reject a policy of extensive nationalization. Speaker after speaker, including the national chairman of the Young Socialists who was present, attacked me for deviationism. Finally I abandoned the arguments on principle which I had felt far freer to advance since my apostasy and suggested that Clause 4 was electorally disastrous and probably not even acceptable to the majority of the members of the Newcastle Labour Club. The next speaker scorned this idea. Had not everyone spoken out against me? He reckoned that I had misjudged the feelings of the meeting as badly as I had misjudged the electorate's likely reaction in Lincoln. I promptly asked the Chairman, Michael Foley, a friend from Lincoln and one of the brightest of my supporters there, to put the matter to the vote. Ten, of whom nine had spoken, voted for Clause 4. The overwhelming majority (none of whom had spoken) voted against it. I doubt whether a year earlier I would have been quite as forthright or as bold. I would have deferred instinctively not only to the likely reactions of my party colleagues but to the party constitution itself.

There seems to me an uncanny parallel between the role of Clause 4 in the Labour Party and that of the Thirty-nine Articles in the Church of England. Most of the clergy (party members) do not believe in the Thirty-nine Articles (Clause 4). They agree that it would be advantageous to the Church (Party) to bring them up to date. But woe betide those who state publicly what is widely agreed in private. The wrath of the fundamentalists will be aroused and for the sake of peace and quiet the majority of churchmen (Party members) even if they have abandoned their fundamentalism long ago, will resent those who are rash enough to tread on sacred ground.*

I remember the 1959 Conference vividly because I had been a candidate in the election in Putney, attended as an *ex officio* delegate and made a speech myself. Gaitskell's speech had shattered the left-wing delegates. It was coolly but politely received at first and then the floodgates burst. Michael Foot (now Member for Ebbw Vale but who had then just lost Devonport) roused the Conference to a fury of opposition, a fury only tempered by a brilliant speech from Charles Pannell, another one from Shirley Williams, and the best speech of all at that Conference, from Denis Healey. I quote, 'What gets cheers at this Conference does not necessarily get votes at elections. If it did, we would have won Devonport.' It was by far the best and toughest speech from him that I have ever heard. I spoke very soon after Gaitskell and defended his projected reforms. There was some booing. *The Economist*, in its issue of December 5th, 1959, referred to the fact that some of the younger Labour candidates shared Gaitskell's views on nationalization, and went on: 'But it was symptomatic of the atmosphere within the Conference hall that when a single one of them, Dick Taverne,

* The parallel with the Church of England might be pushed even farther. One hears the same complaints that not enough people go to church (attend meetings) and that it is particularly difficult to attract the young.

who had fought Putney, spoke up in support of his leader's views (and added sensible observations about ending class warfare within the Party) this was considered an exceptionally courageous thing to do.'

If Gaitskell was disappointed by his reception at the Conference, he was soon forced to realize that he had no hope of carrying the National Executive Committee of the Party. While his strategic analysis had been to my mind impeccable, it was now shown that his tactics had been misguided. You should not raise issues as fundamental as Clause 4 if you cannot win. The majority of the N.E.C. simply would not accept a revision of the constitution. Therefore, partly to avoid a showdown in which he was bound to lose, and partly to preserve his forces for an impending conflict of more immediate and less theoretical significance, Gaitskell withdrew. Nevertheless the episode showed up a weakness in the Party which its subsequent electoral successes in 1964 and 1966 could not entirely conceal. We have not heard the end of Clause 4, as recent events have shown.

The next battle was about unilateral disarmament. As I have already indicated, the left wing supported neutralism. As could be expected, it became closely identified with the Campaign for Nuclear Disarmament, or C.N.D., which argued not only that Britain should abandon her own nuclear weapons, a case which I have always regarded as a strong one, but that Britain should withdraw from a Western alliance in which nuclear weapons played any role. They favoured unilateral abandonment by the West of weapons which the Soviet Union was set on retaining: or as a second best, the withdrawal of Britain from NATO.

It would be inappropriate to go into the merits of the argument in this book. It was perhaps the most important of all the arguments in the 1960s, both because it was concerned with matters of war or peace and because of its impact on the Party. It led to the first major, if temporary, victory of the left wing. It produced the most magnificent political speech of the decade – Gaitskell's speech at the 1960 Party Conference: the 'fight, fight and fight again to save the party that we love' speech. It led to the brief but successful and significant phenomenon of the Campaign for Democratic Socialism, which influenced my own career and my present political attitude. Finally, Gaitskell's defiance and the defeat of the neutralists in 1961, in my view, laid the foundations for Labour's recovery and subsequent victory in 1964.

I should say something about the Campaign for Democratic Socialism, or C.D.S., of which I was Treasurer. After Gaitskell's defeat over Clause 4 it became evident by the middle of 1960 that the neutralists were likely to win the day at the autumn Party Conference. Several of the largest unions had adopted resolutions put forward by C.N.D. Apart from the effect of this on the policies of the Party, increasing left-wing influence within the unions also seemed likely to upset the only basis on which the Labour Party could function constitutionally.

Under the constitution there is an awkward split between power and responsibility. The policy of the Party is officially laid down by the Party Conference and this Conference also elects the National Executive Committee which is the Party's governing body. The unions affiliated to the Party command over four-fifths of the votes at Conference. The Parliamentary Labour Party has no votes, but it does elect the Party's leader and deputy leader who sit on the National Executive Committee. Power, in the sense of the voting power that decides the policy of the Party, therefore rests with the unions. Responsibility on the other hand lies with the Parliamentary Labour Party. When Labour wins an election its leading Members of Parliament constitute the Government. Even in opposition it is the Parliamentary Labour Party which provides the official spokesmen for the Party as a whole and which must determine its own attitude to legislation put forward by the Conservatives.

In the 1940s and 1950s the right-wing union leaders almost automatically supported the Parliamentary leadership with their block votes, much to the consternation of constituency activists. It was hardly democratic, but it made the constitution work because it meant that in practice there was no separation between responsibility and power. However, once left-wing leaders gained control of the block votes and used them to make sure that their own left-wing views became official policy, the position of the Parliamentary Party, at least in opposition and at least while it did not share the left-wing views of the big unions, became a difficult if not untenable one. In 1960 it looked as if the past balance would be upset and as if Party Conference and the Parliamentary Party were heading for a major clash.

By the middle of that year a number of social democrats started to meet together. We were determined to make one last effort to prevent the Party becoming a neo-Marxist Party dedicated to large-scale nationalization at home and neutralism abroad, a Party without hope of recapturing power except in the event of a national catastrophe. We decided to draw up a manifesto and to issue a rallying cry to the moderates and disaffected. We also realized, as the Autumn Party Conference approached, that our future was linked with that of Hugh Gaitskell as he was determined to fight the neutralists at the cost of his position as leader if necessary. Our manifesto was published almost immediately after Gaitskell's defiant 'fight again' speech at the Scarborough Conference.

C.D.S. was launched with this manifesto and it soon attracted a large amount of support from all over Britain. Spurred on by Tony Crosland and efficiently organized by Bill Rodgers, it put like-minded supporters in the constituencies in touch with one another and supplied them with arguments and resolutions. Most important of all, through its supporters in the unions, it campaigned with considerable success to reverse the resolutions of the previous year which had supported unilateral disarmament. We also sought to organize support for the selection of social democrats as Parliamentary candidates, again with a considerable measure of success. I should mention that, although I was Treasurer, my own part in the campaign was a relatively minor one.

In 1961 we saw the fruit of our labours. By a large majority, support for NATO was reaffirmed, C.N.D. was routed and Gaitskell's leadership was finally and firmly secured. Had he lost again, he would have resigned as Leader of the Party despite the support he had from the majority of M.P.s. He realized that while a Labour Government could override Conference decisions, in opposition the Parliamentary Party and Party Conference could not indefinitely propound different policies—a fact which many of the social democrats within the Parliamentary Party seem reluctant to grasp today.

After the 1961 conference C.D.S. flourished for a while, then contracted and early in 1963 was finally dissolved. There were several reasons for this. First, its main task had been accomplished. Secondly, the Common Market issue, which came to the fore in 1962, weakened C.D.S.: most of its members were confirmed and enthusiastic supporters of Britain's entry into the Common Market, but our leader, Hugh Gaitskell, was at first lukewarm and later came out against our entry on the terms then likely to be obtained. Thirdly, we had been formed as a grass roots organization led by non-Parliamentarians and were all the more effective for being outside Parliament. But by 1963 several of our leading members were either in Parliament, like Denis Howell, Bill Rodgers and myself, or had been adopted as candidates and were about to enter, like Brian Walden.

All that remained were close personal friendships and a common bond. There would be occasional old comrades' dinners. They were rather like regimental reunions with recollections of the glorious battles of past campaigns. Several old comrades regretted our disbandment and a number of the Jenkins Group in later years called for the revival of C.D.S. They argued that the left wing, first as Victory for Socialism, and later simply as the Tribune Group, met weekly in the House of Commons to discuss policies and tactics. There was no counterpart on the social democratic side. But C.D.S. was dead, even if its soul went marching on.

The period between 1960 and early 1963 was the only one in recent times when the social democrats have been bold enough to organize as a separate group, even at the risk of committing the unpardonable sin, in the eyes of the loyalists, of being a 'party within a party'. C.D.S. seemed to be a group with considerable appeal to the floating voter. But it is true to say that the reaction of popular opinion was never properly ascertained, as C.D.S. remained an instrument for changing the balance of power in the Party from within, rather than developing as a group appealing directly to opinion outside. The effect of such an appeal remained to be tested.

2

LINCOLN HONEYMOON

Lincoln is a city which captivates most people who become involved with it. Its cathedral, widely regarded—not least by Lincolnians—as the most beautiful in Britain, is perched on a hill and dominates the city and surrounding countryside. Walking or cycling up the High Street on a day with ground mist, you can sometimes see its disembodied towers rise up into the clouds like the towers of a dream city. At night when you see the city from afar, and when the cathedral is floodlit in its full glory, the sight is enough to make a devout believer out of the most sceptical agnostic.

A cathedral city suggests middle-class respectability and garden parties, disturbed only by the influx of cattle from Lincolnshire on market days. Instead, Lincoln is an engineering centre which produces gas turbines, excavators, parts for commercial vehicles, marine diesels and small diesels, grinders and many other products of heavy engineering. It has the feel of an industrial town with its rows of terraced houses at the bottom of the hill. Its personality is split between cathedral and industry. Unfortunately its character has been partly spoiled by the building of several unsightly offices in the centre of the city which obscure many good views of the cathedral. Planning in Lincoln, like planning in Bath, has not been of the quality which Britain's leading historical cities deserve.

It may help to give some more facts about Lincoln. The population within the city boundaries is at present some 74,000, having declined from about 77,000 in the early 1960s, but if one includes the built-up area which continues outwards from the city boundaries, about 100,000 people live in the Lincoln area. The Parliamentary constituency consists of the city only. One local daily paper, the *Lincolnshire Echo*, is delivered into nearly every home in Lincoln; a local weekly paper, the *Lincolnshire Chronicle*, has a circulation within the city of about 8,000. Apart from the national networks, television viewers can receive both Yorkshire and Anglia TV. Lincoln is situated in the East Midlands, 132 miles from London and about 35 miles from the nearest part of the east coast.

There is a certain sense in Lincoln that the city is isolated from the rest of the country, largely because it lies off the main north-south traffic. It has not known the constant migration of workers that swept in and out of other centres in the Midlands. The city has a strong sense of civic pride, accompanied by an even stronger sense of civic pessimism. Half its population seems convinced that in five years Lincoln will be a ghost town and almost resents being told that things may be better than they seem. The inhabitants are conservative in outlook but used to voting Labour in politics. Lincoln people boast that they will not accept outsiders until they have been in Lincoln at least twenty years; but, in fact, they are exceptionally friendly and hospitable. They like to repeat rumours but do not really believe them. They are sceptical, practical, cautious and independent. They believe they are different from everybody else.

Since the war right up to 1973, Lincoln had always returned a Labour Member of Parliament. From 1950 until the end of 1961 the Member of Parliament was Geoffrey (now Sir Geoffrey) de Freitas. He was widely respected by Lincolnians from all Parties, including most of the local Labour Party, but the left-wingers felt that he was remote and regarded him with suspicion. Several of them told me that they thought he was basically a Tory and cited as evidence the fact that he attended the Agricultural Ball. As I found later, these left-wingers believe that it should be the duty of a Labour M.P. to spend most of his time with the Party workers rather than mixing more widely in the constituency.

At the end of 1961 Geoffrey de Freitas was offered by the Conservative Government the post of High Commissioner in

Ghana and accepted. This meant his resignation from Parliament. On the day the announcement was made, I received a telephone call in my chambers in the Temple from John Harris, who was Gaitskell's aide at the time, asking whether I was still interested in standing for Parliament. I had, as already mentioned, stood unsuccessfully in the 1959 election, but was then engaged in building up a practice at the Bar. I said I was interested and was asked to meet Geoffrey de Freitas at the House of Commons. He in turn gave me an introduction to his Party agent in Lincoln.

Gaitskell suggested me for the seat for two reasons; firstly, he was keen to see the leading younger figures of C.D.S. brought into Parliament and Bill Rodgers and myself were the two most obvious candidates. Secondly, it was thought I would be a suitable horse for the Lincoln course. The Labour Party's standing with the public in the aftermath of its bitter wrangles over C.N.D. and Clause 4 was not particularly high. Although Geoffrey de Freitas had retained Lincoln for Labour in the 1959 election by a majority of about 4,400 votes, it was feared that a considerable factor in this victory had been his personal popularity. Without a suitable replacement, very much in Geoffrey's image, the Party was afraid that the seat might even be lost to the Conservatives. It was for this reason that the choice fell on me rather than on Bill Rodgers (who in fact became the Member for Stockton-on-Tees shortly afterwards), as my legal and Oxford background was very similar to Geoffrey's. (During the by-election people even said I looked like Geoffrey!)

The fact that I was an officer of C.D.S., personally recommended to Geoffrey by Hugh Gaitskell and duly selected for the seat, later created a myth about my selection conference that would have given me an honoured place in left-wing demonology even if my more recent clashes with the left wing had never occurred. It is firmly believed by some, and has been reported in the *New Statesman*, that my election was somehow 'rigged' and that I was foisted as a right-winger on an unwilling left-wing local party.* This myth ignores what actually hap-

* See 'London Diary', *New Statesman*, October 29th, 1971.

pened at my election conference and, in particular, what happened at Lincoln.

In the Labour Party the selection of a candidate is made by a General Management Committee, or G.M.C., the governing body of each constituency party. This is composed of delegates from the Wards into which each constituency is divided, and from other affiliated organizations, mainly local branches of Trade Unions. The size of the G.M.C. in Lincoln at the time was about seventy delegates. Nominations for selection can be made by any Ward or affiliated organization. The Executive Committee—elected from the G.M.C. delegates—then draws up a short list from those nominated, and at by-elections does so in the presence of the Regional Organizer of the Labour Party. The final choice is made by the G.M.C. after it has heard each short-listed candidate speak and answer questions for half an hour. It should be clear from this account that no one can be selected as candidate unless he wins a majority of the votes of the G.M.C. If the G.M.C. does not like a candidate, it need not have him. What is more, local parties are very sensitive to any attempt to have a candidate imposed on them by the official Party machine, and once it is known that someone is the favourite of Transport House (Labour's national headquarters) he is at a major disadvantage.

It is true that in winning the nomination at Lincoln I did get some help from C.D.S. (apart from being recommended by Hugh Gaitskell). We had one sole C.D.S. member in Lincoln, Ken Rawding, but he was a man of some influence; he was a former Party Chairman and Treasurer and at the time he was Chairman of the Education Committee of the local Lincoln City Council. (After my break with the Labour Party he became the Treasurer of the Lincoln Democratic Labour Association.) I met him before the selection conference and he briefed me on the local scene. He also put in a good word for me with those of the G.M.C. who sympathized with C.D.S. But the most important contact was Geoffrey de Freitas himself, who supported C.D.S., and his agent Vic Phillips, to whom Geoffrey introduced me. Vic took me to visit several Party members.

Some of these agreed to support me and I was duly nominated by one of the Constituency Wards.

In 1962 the Lincoln Constituency Party was fairly evenly balanced between the Gaitskellites and the left wing. The Gaitskellites had a small majority on the G.M.C. and also on the Executive Committee, while the left wing, then mainly identified with the Campaign for Nuclear Disarmament, held the chairmanship in the person of Ralph Wadsworth, an important character in this story.

I was later told that the Gaitskellite majority on the Executive Committee used its votes quite ruthlessly to limit the short list to four anti-unilateralist moderates. One of them, Terry Boston, later withdrew because he was likely to become the candidate for Faversham. The other three were Arthur Bottomley, Niall MacDermot and myself. Bottomley had been Member of Parliament for Rochester and Chatham and a Minister in the 1945–51 Government. He was later Member of Parliament for Middlesborough East and became a Minister in the Wilson Government. Niall MacDermot had been Member of Parliament for Lewisham North until the 1959 election. He later became Member of Parliament for Derby North and Financial Secretary to the Treasury. Niall MacDermot had most nominations, while I had only one. No full-blooded Socialist C.N.D. left-winger was allowed on the short list, and the left wing of the constituency Party, perhaps understandably since they formed a substantial minority, resented the fact that a choice between Bottomley, MacDermot and myself was to them politically a choice between Tweedledum, Tweedledee and their triplet brother.

The selection conference itself proved to be a portent of things to come. I made my speech and answered questions about C.N.D., nationalization and the Common Market. I made it clear that I was against the first, lukewarm about the second and in favour of the third. I believe the other two were asked similar questions and gave similar answers. While they both had the benefit of experience, I had the benefit of youth (I was then thirty-three years old) and I was selected easily on the first ballot. The most significant development was, however, that after the questions and before the votes, Leo Beckett, who turned out to be the real leader of the left wing in Lincoln, walked out of the selection conference with three of his colleagues. He explained later that this was not personal antipathy but a protest about the kind of views expressed by all three candidates. In the euphoria of victory the incident seemed to me of no importance at the time.

Shortly after my adoption, I started on a round of ward meetings as is the custom for new candidates. The first of these was the Annual General Meeting of what was then much the largest and important ward, Ermine Ward. It has since been split up. This was clearly Beckett territory, with Leo in the Chair and his wife as Secretary. Previously the ward had sent a politically mixed bag of delegates to the G.M.C. What I now witnessed was the execution of a carefully prepared and totally successful left-wing coup. Names were moved and voted on for delegates to the G.M.C., and the votes fell into two groups: one group received thirteen votes each; the other group received three. Amongst the second group, who were not elected, was Eric Richardson, a highly influential Gaitskellite who was absent from the ward meeting. He was a former Chairman of the Party and had been Niall MacDermot's principal backer. It seemed he had been held mainly responsible for the strong-arm tactics of the Executive Committee and indeed this may have done something to prejudice Niall MacDermot's candidature. Later I inquired of the agent what these votes implied. He confirmed my fears. The left wing had taken revenge for their defeat at the short-listing of candidates and had made an example of one of the most uncompromising of their opponents. They had, at a stroke, swung the balance of the G.M.C. their way.

Had I not been totally absorbed in preparation for the by-election, I suppose I might have acted to mobilize the Centre and Right at this stage. But I had hardly been adopted. Nor was it the most propitious moment for bitter in-fighting, since Lincoln's by-election was viewed as of some importance by the national press and had become the centre of their attentions. So the battlefield was surrendered to the left wing without a shot fired. Later it did not seem a matter of life and death, as none worked harder at the by-election than the Becketts or Ralph Wadsworth.

I was, however, from the moment of my adoption by the Lincoln Labour Party in an unusual position. Most M.P.s and their local parties work in close harmony; few of them certainly find themselves with a management committee that is totally out of sympathy with their political views. In my case I was a Gaitskellite and social democratic M.P. who had been introduced to Lincoln because of the part I played in fighting the left wing in C.D.S. I faced a G.M.C. that was not just left-wing, but dominated by a small group of very determined left-wingers who knew what they were doing—fighting for power in the Party, locally and nationally against people like myself. Lincoln was, therefore, a test-bed for the conflict between the two opposite factions of the Labour Party.

As personalities play some part in this story, this may be an appropriate place to give a thumbnail sketch of some of the *dramatis personae*.

Leo Beckett was throughout a central figure. He is an engineer, a member of the Amalgamated Engineering Union Workers and holds the job of Foreman in the Research Department of G.E.C., Lincoln's biggest employers. He was then in his mid-thirties and still looks far younger than he is. His three most obvious qualities are personality, intelligence and idealism.

There can be no doubt about the force of his personality. Most of the time he is charming, cheerful, considerate, gregarious, warm and witty. Most people, from young children to the elderly, found him very good company. His mouth turns up at the corners. This gives the impression that he is smiling, even when he is not, and leads some of his opponents to think of him as a hypocrite who pretends goodwill when he is burning with antipathy. One of my correspondents once described his smile, as seen on a controversial television programme, as 'vulpine'.

When roused, he displays a command of passionate and sustained invective which would be the envy of a Savanarola. If one shared his views these outbursts would seem magnificent. If one happens to be the object of his fury one has a sense of some discomfort.

Leo undervalues his own intelligence. Had he not done so persistently, he might well have been an outstanding left-wing M.P. Leo would be surprised at this assessment of his abilities. Admittedly his intelligence is not applied to the logical analysis of ideas, or the careful marshalling of facts. It is intuitive rather than logical. He distrusts intellectuals. He is also a formidable organizer.

As for his idealism, he is wholly, passionately, devotedly concerned to further the cause of Socialism as he sees it, which is in very fundamentalist terms. He walks, talks, breathes, lives politics, twenty-four hours a day. The Cause is the working class (especially the British working class), who are, as he sees it, oppressed by the capitalist system, exploited by capitalist bosses and from time to time betrayed by middle-class Labour Ministers. If only they were given a proper lead by a proper Socialist Labour Party, a militant working class would vote to a man for full-scale nationalization, for workers' control of industry, and the abolition of the profit motive from our present society. He is convinced that the Labour Party is the proper instrument for this change and gives the Party (that is its Conference and 'rank and file') an almost religious loyalty. Although a devoted adherent of the Campaign for Nuclear Disarmament, he once said that if the C.N.D. was proscribed and he was forced to choose between C.N.D. and the Labour Party, he would have felt bound to abandon C.N.D. One of his less attractive features is that he shares with many of the extreme Left a readiness to use almost any methods to further his ends and that he is always ready to detect conspiracies around him. He 'organizes', but his opponents 'plot'. He is inclined to feel that if you do not agree with his views, your motives must be suspect.

Leo's mixture of force of personality, powers of persuasion and idealism has brought many recruits into the Lincoln Labour

Party's ranks and many of them were soon converted to his own brand of Socialism. His total dedication to Party work soon gave him effective control over the Party's organization.

The second lead was played by Ralph Wadsworth, a draughtsman who is about the same age as Leo. He was, as I have stated, Chairman of the Party when I arrived and remained so for several years afterwards. He was a local Councillor and was Chairman of the Council's Planning Committee. Later he relinquished his post in the Party, but became Mayor and Leader of the Labour Group on the Council. I shall not describe him at length as I have never found him a congenial person. It is a pity that he, and not Leo, became Leader of the Labour Council, as Leo might well have shown an imagination and an enlightenment in his approach to planning and the management of the City's affairs of which Ralph Wadsworth was incapable. Leo, however, always preferred to concentrate on the Party and to remain behind the scenes, although he did agree to become Party Chairman in 1971.

Ralph Wadsworth is certainly a man of ability and strong character. I always get the impression that his influence over Party members, particularly his colleagues on the Council, was based on their fear rather than affection, fear of his tongue and his ability to use power. He knows how to handle committees, speaks well and argues more logically than most of his political colleagues. He wanted to be a Member of Parliament and was for a time on the Candidates' List at Transport House, though he was never adopted in any constituency. He once said he would like to have been Member of Parliament for Lincoln, but his role in helping to oust me disqualified him, he felt, from seeking the candidature on his own home ground. His views are orthodox Tribune Left.

Finally, there was my second Agent, Pat Mulligan, who succeeded Vic Phillips about a year after my arrival, when Vic most unfortunately resigned for personal reasons. Vic was a great loss because of his loyalty and steadiness, qualities which it is easy to underrate. I was very lax about the appointment of Pat Mulligan, taking it on trust from Leo, with whom I was then on good terms, and Ralph that he was the right person to be considered. I failed to make inquiries, as I should have done, about his political past. I would have found strong left-wing connections, and I have no doubt that this is why Leo and Ralph proposed him to the Executive Committee. The fact is that he was the only applicant with obvious experience as an Agent who seemed worth interviewing. I liked him on interview. In fact I got on with him pretty well for the next seven years. Ron Hayward once told me, when he was still National Agent for the Labour Party, that in the days before the Common Market clash, he used to regard us as personifying the ideal relationship between Agent and Member of Parliament.

Pat Mulligan is a smallish, bearded Scot with a glass eye. He was inefficient on occasions, but then so was I. He did not always keep me in the picture about what was going on. I still do not believe that this was intentional, although some of my Lincoln friends warned me many years ago not to trust him because of his left-wing sympathies and associates. But Pat was certainly deeply concerned about people. He seemed to be almost entirely dedicated to securing the success of the Party and my return at the next election.

Emotionally he was a fundamentalist Socialist like Leo, but intellectually he seemed to understand the difficulties of exercising power in a rough and unkind world. Pat was eager to broaden the base of the Lincoln Party and was at one time accused of bringing in too many intellectuals: we had one doctor, one architect and one biochemist active in our ranks—which just about summed up our membership from the ranks of the professions.

The shock of the Labour Government's defeat in the General Election in 1970 seemed to drive Pat back into the womb of his earlier class-based Socialism. Throughout, he alone of the leading figures in the local party was consistently hostile to the Common Market and after 1970 he was passionately so. To him, Britain's entry on any terms represented a betrayal of Socialism, a denial of all he had ever stood for. The Common Market was the institutionalized embodiment of capitalism. It was a creation of the market economy on an international scale and he was convinced that if the captains of industry supported it, as they did, this must be because it would preclude for ever the establishment of a Socialist state. He soon convinced himself that he was being asked to act as the lapdog of a rebellious M.P. who was working against a policy which the rank and file had taken to their hearts and who was actually supporting the hated Tories. Our personal relations deteriorated rapidly and at the end became the more bitter because they had previously been close. He supported those who were seeking to remove the Member of Parliament whose cause he was supposed to support.

In my early years at Lincoln, relations with the Party were reasonably happy ones, all things considered. The by-election had been a great success in which we had won by a majority of 7,000 votes, the largest-ever majority for Labour in Lincoln. We won the General Election of 1964 with a smaller majority (4,600), but everyone basked happily in the sunshine of a Labour Government. Those were the early days of so-called purposive government, in which the legacy left by the Tories had first to be cleared away, but in due course we all felt certain cornucopia would be at hand. We would see a rapid rate of economic growth, reforms and measures to help the working man, especially the lower-paid. It seemed awkward and sometimes embarrassing that C.N.D. and the Victory for Socialism Group were in a majority on the G.M.C. at Lincoln. But I had no worries about my own position. In those days the lion really did seem to lie down with the lamb—the bitter clashes of C.N.D. and the Gaitskellites were almost the distant memories of a past best forgotten. Indeed, C.D.S. had been disbanded in 1963. There were some rumblings at my meetings with my Constituency Party because Britain still had nuclear weapons, and there was understandable opposition to the uncritical support by the Labour Government of U.S. policy in Vietnam. But when I defended the policies of the Government against attack, these were minor domestic tiffs, or so they seemed then. True, some of the Old Guard who used to form the majority of the

Lincoln Labour Party warned me from time to time that the left wing were waiting for an opportunity to oust me, that they had never yet forgotten the selection conference: I regarded this as alarmist and thought their fears were based on chagrin.

3

MINISTER

In the 1966 election Labour won a great victory with an overall majority of 97 seats. I myself was promoted to office. I first became Parliamentary Under-Secretary at the Home Office; in April 1968 I was moved up to become Minister of State at the Treasury; and from September 1969 until our defeat in the election of 1970, I was Financial Secretary to the Treasury. Ironically the moment of Party triumph and personal promotion was the time when my constituency troubles really began. Partly this was due to the very fact that I became a Minister, partly because disillusionment with the Labour Government in the next four years was nowhere felt more keenly than amongst the left-wing activists of the Lincoln party.

There is no evidence that M.P.s enhance their position in their constituencies by becoming Ministers. This may seem surprising. It is on the face of it a sign of recognition of worth by the leader of the faithful. Indeed it is often (less often perhaps than the outsider assumes) a reward for intelligence or standing in the Party, or assiduity in Parliament. Constituencies like to think that they have a Member of Parliament of some distinction, and going round constituencies I have often heard the view that their particular Member of Parliament ought to be in the Cabinet. (Although the general reputation of politicians is low, it is surprising how many people exempt their own M.P. from the general censure.)

But the evidence from past elections suggests that at a time of popular reaction against a government, Ministers may suffer particularly badly. In 1964 Ministers like Henry Brooke and Geoffrey Rippon suffered swings against themselves personally which were well above the average swing against the Conservatives nationally. Certainly I can think of no case where former Ministers did particularly well. There are reasons for this.

A Minister finds that—offsetting the advantage of recognition, or status, or prestige—he loses one of the most valuable prerogatives of the M.P., the right to criticize his own Government for policies which seem to affect his constituency adversely. For instance, when I explained to a group of constituents that I could not oppose the particular Bill which they thought affected their interests adversely, and said that because I was a member of the Government which promoted the Bill I had to accept collective responsibility, I was told, 'We elected you to represent us and not to be a Minister.' The Minister cannot ask parliamentary questions, only answer them. He cannot raise any constituency matter on the floor of the House.

In my case, no issue brought out more clearly the conflict between Constituency interests and Ministerial office than a closure of one of Lincoln's factories which happened while I was a Treasury Minister. Foster Gwynnes of Lincoln had been taken over some years before by Allens of Bedford and became Allen Gwynnes. The Lincoln factory made pumps. In 1968, in the interests of rationalization, the new management decided that all the work should be shifted to Bedford. About four hundred men would lose their jobs in Lincoln. I was immediately called in to help by local Union leaders. I argued the matter with Sir Kenneth Allen, Chairman of the Allen Gwynnes Board, and a deputation from Lincoln met Sir Kenneth and his colleagues in London. We found the management had made up their minds irrevocably. 'We are only doing', Sir Kenneth replied to me, 'what you in the Treasury and your colleagues in Government have told us to do—we are rationalizing and making ourselves more competitive.' As a final fling, Union leaders in Lincoln arranged for a protest march of all those affected by the closure through the city. This was at least partly a protest against Government policy for encouraging mergers and rationalization and the 'shake-out', as Harold Wilson had called it. I was asked if I would march at the head of the column. As a

Treasury Minister, I had to refuse; but my absence was noted and resented.

In addition to this conflict of loyalties for a Minister, there is likely to be a conflict of engagements.

I think many Ministers in fact take too many engagements on themselves and do not leave enough time for reflection. However, they cannot avoid a number of official engagements; nor should they avoid speaking engagements throughout the country on behalf of the Party or the Government. I think I did my fair share of these. But if things are not happy in your own home base, you soon hear rumours of discontent that the Member is spending too much time wandering all over the country and not enough time with his own party workers. 'Our M.P. is too busy being a Minister and is losing touch.'

By the end of July 1966, less than four months after the great election victory, there were local complaints that the Government had forgotten what it had been elected for.

I shall not attempt to evaluate the achievements of the Labour Government. I am concerned here only with the impact of its actions on members of the Lincoln Labour Party. They had little to cheer about, and this did not apply only to those who were militant Socialists looking impatiently for signs of an instant and total transformation of our society and the vindication of the working class. There were very few measures from the 1966 Government which they could regard as socialist. Our programme of social reform, particularly the housing programme, suffered heavily from the long struggle to right the balance of payments. Perhaps our most radical reforms were the changes in our social laws, like the reform of laws against homosexuals and against abortion. Although I was partly concerned with these when I was a Minister at the Home Office, they were of no interest to most of the members of my G.M.C. I remember at one G.M.C. meeting, a Councillor declaring his exasperation that the House of Commons 'spent all its time debating Bills for homosexuals when they should be discussing unemployment every night'.

In retrospect I am amazed how much active Labour Party

members tolerated. They loathed the Labour Government's support of the Americans in Vietnam, and no number of Conference decisions denouncing it made any difference to the Labour Government's foreign policy. Indeed I must confess, to some extent with hindsight, that most of the social democrats in the party were too uncritical of their Government's Vietnam policy. I believe that they over-reacted against the violent criticism of American actions mainly because the previous argument with the left wing over foreign policy had been about the need for collective defence in support of the Atlantic Alliance. It seemed to follow that not only the alliance but the actions of our principal ally should be defended. In the event, many supporters of the Western alliance were themselves more ready to defend American policy than were their friends in the United States. It was rather like the over-reaction of Anglophiles in the United States about a decade before, who, to the chagrin of their friends in the United Kingdom, felt bound to support the Anglo-French invasion of Suez.

Next, the militants on the Left were outraged by Wilson's denunciation of 'the tightly knit group of politically motivated men' behind the seamen's strike which took place in the summer of 1966. No one should underestimate the instinctive sympathy which the left wing feel for workers who go on strike, wherever they may be and whatever the justification for the strike (or lack of it). They feel sure that the cause must be just. They regard it as self-evident that Socialists and workers should show solidarity with those who have denied themselves their wages in the fight against the enemy, the employer. In fact they feel something of the call to the barricades in every strike. Yet now they were told by their own leader that it was all a Communist plot. The shock was considerable.

More serious, because more widespread amongst all ranks of Labour Party workers, not just the left wing, was the slow undermining of morale caused by the wages freeze of 1966 and the tough Incomes Policy that followed in 1967. When, as head of the new Department of Economic Affairs, George Brown first announced the Incomes Policy in 1965, it seemed acceptable in principle and even popular. Its apparent popularity was misleading because people were always more ready to apply it to others than to themselves.

However, the Incomes Policy was bound to become unpopular when Wilson and Callaghan decided against devaluation in July 1966 and opted instead for deflation and a wages freeze. It was to have been a policy for the planned growth of wages. Instead it became the main instrument for holding down wages as part of a deflationary policy. As a result it became discredited, and whatever its economic benefits for the country as a whole, it had a disastrous effect on trade union elections. Moderate union leaders who supported the policy were soon in great difficulties. I suspect the Incomes Policy was the main reason for the election of Hugh Scanlon as President of the Amalgamated Engineering Union.

Any policy which calls for restraint and depends at the same time on goodwill and consent faces obvious difficulties. There will always be people who argue that sacrifices are totally unnecessary, and sometimes they will be right. The Opposition, says one school of thought, has a duty to oppose. Oppose the Tories duly did, claiming that with better management, in one way or another, Government interference in private wage-bargaining could be avoided. They were very careful not to spell out specific alternatives. They would certainly have no truck with devaluation. In fact they even opposed the belated devaluation when it finally came.

The Conservative case against the Incomes Policy seemed the more plausible because it found an echo in the denunciation of the policy by the Labour Party's own left wing. Although they start from an entirely different point of view, the left wing often end up with much the same conclusions as the right wing of the Conservative Party. Enoch Powell and Michael Foot have not only stood shoulder to shoulder over Europe. They combined against reform of the House of Lords. Above all, they marched side by side through the lobbies against the Incomes Policy and deployed astonishingly similar arguments, namely that it was not part of the Government's role to restrict the traditional freedom of the trade unions to bargain for their members.

It is not surprising that the ordinary working man, told by the Right and the far Left that he was being asked to bear an unfair burden, felt at the least bewildered by what the Government was doing and at the worst betrayed. Throughout 1967 local Labour parties became more and more hostile to the actions of the Labour Government. Some of the by-elections at which I spoke and canvassed that year (especially the north-east Leicester by-election where the Government suffered a shattering defeat) gave me the most depressing experiences of my political life because the mood on the doorstep was so unfriendly. The landslide to the Tories in the local elections in the spring of 1967 completed the demoralization of local party workers. Ralph Wadsworth, who always saw things in terms of local elections, bitterly complained at one G.M.C. meeting, 'I only hope people at the top realize what they have done to us on the Council.'

One blow followed another. In January 1968, after devaluation had finally been forced on the Labour Government, there were large-scale cuts in programmes for public spending. One of the ways in which the spending of the Ministry of Health was cut back was by restoring the prescription charges which in 1964 the Labour Government had abolished to the cheers of its supporters. Restoring charges was a symbolic slaughter of the sacred cow, deliberately intended to underline the seriousness of the situation. The Lincoln G.M.C. duly reacted like Hindus whose religion has been outraged. Some of the meetings of the General Management Committee during this period were extremely difficult. Leo Beckett bitterly denounced me for failing to resign from Wilson's Government. No self-respecting Socialist, he felt, could remain a member of it. 'We don't want a cabbage as our M.P.,' he said. I also learnt from the Regional Organizer of the Labour Party, Jim Cattermole, in April 1968, that on one of his visits to Lincoln Leo asked him, 'How can we get rid of our Member of Parliament?'

His grounds were that no one who supported the Wilson Government could be acceptable to the Lincoln Party.

This happened in fact a week before I left the Home Office and became Minister of State at the Treasury. But the majority group on the G.M.C. were not impressed by this promotion. The Treasury is, after all, the department blamed by many in the Labour Party for sabotaging the good intentions of Labour Governments. When the Department of Economic Affairs was set up in 1964 by Wilson and Brown, this was in part a move to limit the influence of the Treasury. When the Department of Economic Affairs was abolished again in 1969, all the worst fears of the left wing about the irresistibility of the Treasury's power seemed to be confirmed. Anyway, becoming a Treasury Minister meant a far more personal identification with the unpopular measures of the Government than a post in the Home Office had been. Before, I had only been associated with the policies—now I was directly responsible.

Early in 1969 came what they regarded as the final betrayal: the publication of a White Paper called *In Place of Strife* which contained the Labour Government's proposals for reforming industrial relations. These went much farther than the recommendations of the Royal Commission which Wilson had originally set up, and proposed amongst other things fines for unconstitutional strikes in breach of negotiated agreements, and a Governmental power to enforce a 'reconciliation pause' before a strike could legally take place. The story of these proposals has been told by Peter Jenkins in *The Battle of Downing Street.* Wilson had become convinced that our economic well-being demanded action against unofficial strikes, and he and Barbara Castle were at first quite prepared to battle it out with the unions.

First reactions to the White Paper in Lincoln gave no hint of the violent feelings that it later aroused. I expounded its proposals to my Executive Committee in February 1969, soon after it was published, and was almost surprised at the apparent absence of dissent. The bulk of the document was accepted; the controversial parts were mildly questioned. I suspect that if the Government had pushed their plans through quickly, a Bill to enact the proposals might have been passed. Instead they delayed. In Lincoln a degree of opposition built up among shop stewards of all shades of militancy, and amongst reasonable trade union officials as well, which surprised me by its intensity. By June it was clear to me that if Lincoln reactions were anything to go by, we faced our deepest split yet and one from which the Party might not recover. For Labour Party supporters this was the last straw: as they saw it, the Government had attacked the standards of living of the working class for the sake of the balance of payments and restricted the bargaining power of the trade unions by a statutory incomes policy; now, they were convinced, the very right to strike was threatened. They would fight the Government's plans to the bitter end and no longer cared whether this opposition meant the end of any chances of victory for Labour at the next election. Most of them thought the next election was lost in any event. Nationally the picture was much the same. I do not blame Harold Wilson for retreating in the face of overwhelming odds and abandoning his Bill. I do blame him for not having stopped running ever since. The whole venture was a disaster. The confidence of the militants in their own power was enhanced; the confidence of the public in the ability of the Government to deal with the unions was totally destroyed.

After the Government had abandoned the controversial sections of *In Place of Strife*, morale improved throughout the Party. By the middle of 1969 the balance of payments became favourable and with the recovery of our trade balance came a national recovery in the Labour Party's fortunes. But when I look back at this dark period of the Labour Government and the effect on party workers in Lincoln, three points seem to me to stand out.

First, it is ironic in retrospect that one of its actions which might have been as controversial as the rest, namely the decision to apply for entry to the Common Market in 1967, caused very little opposition. The Lincoln Party knew I was strongly in favour. I came across no strong feelings against.

Next, I must confess considerable sympathy with the frustrations of people who expected so much from our big majority in 1966 and, in the event, were given so little. They expected too much, but this was partly because they had been promised too much. One hopes future Governments of the Left will promise less and achieve more.

Lastly, there is no doubt that widespread and bitter disillusionment with the Labour Government left the militant Left more dominant on the Lincoln General Management Council than ever before. Gradually more and more of the loyalists, those whose instincts were to defend the Government rather than attack it, became fed up and retired. It took courage to stand up at G.M.C. meetings and speak out against the prevailing mood. One of the few prepared to do so was Roy Lilley, then District Secretary of the Amalgamated Engineering Union, a man whose courage was quite exceptional.*

Ken Rawding, my original C.D.S. contact, had been forced to retire from active politics some time before because of promotion at work. His sister, Flossie Poucher, and her husband Walt (two excellent political organizers) were some of the few who did not give up the fight. We used to derive mutual support from meetings at their house with a hard core of loyalists from their Ward. I also had the good fortune to stay frequently with two people who became the closest personal friends, John and Clodagh Wilkinson (later Councillor Mrs Wilkinson), who provided a home from home for me (and for the rest of the family when they came up to Lincoln) and who gave the strongest possible moral support during the many ups and downs of those years.

* It was Roy Lilley who stopped the engineering strike in 1968 singlehanded by bringing an action in the High Court for an injunction against Hugh Scanlon on the grounds that the decision to strike had been taken in contravention of proper union procedure. I still believe that by his action he saved Britain from an appalling economic crisis and the Labour Government from obliteration. A strike in the autumn of 1968, when we were still a long way from a stable balance of payments surplus and when the pound was under severe pressure, could have had totally disastrous results. Roy Lilley also paid the price. When he stood for the National Executive of his Union a year later, the leaders of the A.E.U. pulled out all the stops to see he was defeated. As his candidature had meant his giving up the post of District Secretary, he was left unemployed; he then found employers to whom he applied more ready with words of appreciation than offers of a job.

The political sympathies of the G.M.C. can be best shown by referring to the list of guests invited to annual dinners, special meetings and May Day rallies between 1966 and 1970. They read like a roll-call of the leading figures from the Tribune Group: Norman Atkinson, Ian Mikardo, John Horner, John Mendelson, Stan Newens, as well as Ernie Roberts, a very left-wing officer of the A.E.U. The M.P.s were all rebels against the Incomes Policy and almost every other aspect of the Government's economic policy. Indeed, four of them voted with the Tories against the Government on a Three-Line Whip, an action which had hitherto been regarded as the ultimate crime against Party discipline. This only enhanced their virtues in the eyes of their Lincoln hosts. One of my right-wing friends complained after one May Day meeting at Grafton House that it was more like a Communist Party than a Labour Party rally. Knowing the views of some of the speakers I avoided appearing on the same platform in order to avoid a row.

Again the resolutions sent annually by the Lincoln Party to the National Conference of the Labour Party reflected their disaffection with the policies of the Labour Government. This can best be seen in their 1965 and 1966 resolutions on foreign policy:

> This Conference feels compelled by events to note that Socialist principles of foreign policy have been jettisoned one after another by the Government in favour of a continuation of the policy of the Conservative Party and the previous Government. Any outstanding breach of election pledges and of clearly stated policy is that of the discarding of any attempt to bring forward a scheme for a nuclear free zone in Europe and instead, the pursuit of the exact opposite. This is not only in complete disregard of the Labour Party's pledges and promised policies but is leading rapidly to a deteriorating situation in Europe. Another example of failure to attempt a Social foreign policy is the unvarying and unquestioning support in any and every circumstance of the United States' activities in Vietnam.

It is now abundantly clear that the cost of pursuing a non-Socialist foreign policy is a major source of economic disability to the country as a whole and that continuing the Conservative foreign policy must, at the least, delay or even destroy the basis for a Socialist programme at home, and at the worst, may well involve us in a war as completely disastrous as it would be unnecessary.

Conference therefore demands of the Government that foreign policy shall be based on Socialist principles and that election pledges and promised policies shall be treated seriously and as having meaning and purpose. (1965)

This Conference calls upon the Government to dissociate Britain completely from the U.S. Government's policy in Vietnam. (1966)

The 1967 resolution concentrated on the importance of Conference:

This Conference whilst recognising that the Government has to take executive decisions and that the Labour Party owes a loyalty to the Government, nevertheless suggests that loyalty is a two-way relationship. The Government thus owes a loyalty—not necessarily to individuals—but to Labour Party principles.

The essence of this resolution is to remind the Government that Annual Conference is the only effective instrument for giving expression to the aims and aspirations of the Labour National Executive Committee, to implement those resolutions instructing the Parliamentary Labour Party as to their action in the House of Commons, and to give immediate effect to the policies as laid down in the 1964 and 1966 Election manifestoes.

I think it was a sense of futility about the impact of Conference resolutions which upset the left-wing activists as much as anything—hence the demand that Conference resolutions should be obeyed by the Government. This demand was ignored as much as any other. Here they were, as they saw it, holding up the flag of Socialism amidst the jeers of their workmates and the indifference or hostility of the electorate, wearing out their shoe-leather on the doorstep at local elections in which the Tories swept to power in the Lincoln Guildhall, often volunteering to canvass in by-elections elsewhere in the country where huge swings would be recorded against the Labour Government. Yet when they came to exercise their democratic rights to express their views, and to formulate policy through resolutions submitted to the Party's Annual Conference, the Government simply pushed them aside. They were cannon fodder and no more, allowed no say in the strategy of the war that caused such heavy casualties. No wonder they felt bolshy.

On the whole my local arguments in Lincoln were impersonal. Except when I was being accused of behaving 'like a cabbage' because I did not resign, my personal relations with the leading figures of the Party were, in general, civilized. Not that my arguments had any effect. I would ask them whether they thought that the leaders they had trusted in the Opposition, including the left-wing leaders whom they voted to power on the National Executive, were now knaves or fools? Was it not at least possible that they were neither, that the difficulties we faced were greater than we expected, that we could not ignore our creditors abroad, that we could not simply ask the balance of payments problem to go away, that we could start to make real progress only after the country had a strong balance of payments, etc., etc.? They would not actually argue against me. They would rather treat me the way the Government treated Conference resolutions: ignore what I said.

I could only come to meetings of the Management Committee occasionally, as they were held in the middle of the week, which made it almost impossible for me to attend. What did become noticeable to me was a growing feeling of class resentment. People could not understand how it was that the working class did not fare better under a Labour Government and they explained this in terms of the leadership of the Party being middle-class or corrupted by the middle-class environment in which Ministers move. This class prejudice in a part of the Labour Party is a curious phenomenon because of its obvious double standards. Ray Gunter, for example, the Minister for Labour (and later Minister for Power), was totally working-class in his background and outlook and sympathy. When he resigned he wanted to return 'to the folk from whence he came'. (I think it is true that the Cabinet was weaker when neither Ray Gunter nor George Brown was any longer in it – their instinctive feeling for working-class reactions was badly missed.) Yet Ray Gunter was bitterly hated by the left wing because of his views, especially because he spoke out against strikes. Tom Driberg on the other hand was a public school boy, but he is a favourite of the left wing, regularly voted on to the constituency section of the National Executive Committee because his views are left-wing. On the face of it one would expect views, not class background, to be the criterion. Yet if someone combines the two crimes of not being left-wing and being middle-class, then his views are held to be entirely due to his class background! What was particularly disturbing was that Pat Mulligan, my Agent, despite his general desire to see the Government returned, began to show strong signs of his class prejudice at times of stress.

As the 1970 election drew nearer, the ranks closed, the wounds seemed to heal and we seemed to rediscover a common purpose. When the election was announced, we knew we were going to win again in Lincoln. We were also sure Labour would win again in the country. Morale was once again high. In any event the election campaign itself binds together all Party workers, unless something goes drastically wrong. In Lincoln nothing went wrong. If Labour had won again, as was then widely expected, I suspect this book would never have been written. As things turned out, we did reasonably well in Lincoln, winning by 4,720 votes after a 2·3 per cent swing against us since the 1966 election. But the national swing against Labour was 4·7 per cent and the Tories won a majority of thirty seats. On the night of the election it became clear that I could soon be facing formidable difficulties.

4

SHOWDOWN

Few nights are as black as the night when a General Election is lost. If you lose your own seat at the same time, the feeling must be suicidal. If things seem to go well, the final period of an election can produce a kind of drunkenness. You no longer see things in perspective. Obviously you believe that victory for your party will be good for the country at all times; but by then your own party's programme and the other side's present a glaring contrast of black and white. Optimism affects even candidates who clearly have no chance. When the polls seemed to confirm the emphatic reports of our own canvassers in Lincoln, and with our meetings well attended throughout, I was as sure as sure could be that I was heading for a record majority in Lincoln and the Labour Party was heading for its third victory in a row. Then the count and the early results and the moment of truth. My majority was cut by over 2,000. The early results clearly showed that Labour was losing. Janice and I retired with our friends to Grafton House, where people were drinking beer and staring gloomily at the television. We sat numbed, watching one disastrous loss follow another. Suddenly Leo Beckett whirled round and said bitingly, 'This is all the fault of prescription charges and the attack on the unions. I knew it would happen. The people won't stand for it.'

It would not be fair to argue with his particular selection of the causes of Labour's failure. They are significant only because they illustrate the view generally accepted on the Left that Labour wins, not by persuading the floating voter, but by firing its natural supporters with sufficient enthusiasm to bring them in masses to the polls. He clearly felt, as others have argued since, that our defeat was caused by the disillusionment of Party workers and abstentions by Labour voters. In fact there was a 76 per cent poll in the 1966 election and a 72 per cent poll in 1970. The 5 per cent swing against Labour was, on the face of it, due mainly not to abstentions but to a sizeable switch in allegiance.

The ominous part of Leo's outburst was less its content than its tone. Within a few hours of the closing of the polling booths all the goodwill towards the leadership and the sense of unity which had been built up again during the period before the election and in the election itself had vanished. All the bitterness of the long years of crisis of 1966–9 had welled up again In the Lincoln Labour Party it now seemed only too likely that the left wing would seek revenge on the milk-and-water Socialists who had dominated the years of the Wilson Government.

I could see clearly, even at that time, that my biggest problem would be British entry to the Common Market. Many of us who belonged to the Labour Committee for Europe also saw it as the most difficult issue that the Parliamentary Party would be facing in the first few years of opposition.

We feared not only that the Party would turn against the Market but that we might face a split as serious as that of 1960 over nuclear disarmament. Only this time the odds would be against the Social Democrats. The centre would follow the leader, and I, for one, thought it likely that he would vote against entry.* We knew that it would be most unlikely that terms acceptable to a Tory Government would not be acceptable to us. So we had to face the likelihood of voting against official Party policy.

I also knew that this would place me in a particularly difficult position with the Lincoln Party. At this stage I had not fully thought out all the consequences and certainly did not consider the possibility of standing as an independent, let alone at a by-election. Although I realized that my future would be at risk, I had not fully considered what to do if things went wrong. As far as I can recall my thoughts at the time—and it is difficult to keep recollections entirely free from the distortion caused by later developments—there were two considerations which in-

* See Chapter 8.

fluenced me. The first was a misplaced confidence that somehow all would be all right on the night. It has rarely happened that an M.P. has been disowned by his constituency party. The last case had been that of Mrs Margaret Mackay, disowned by her constituency in 1970 for her passionate dedication to the Arab cause. At the time I thought those circumstances were unique. (This is, of course, what they later said about Lincoln.) When, in the past, Tory M.P.s were dismissed by their parties for holding unpopular minority opinions, like Nigel Nicolson at Bournemouth on the issues of capital punishment and the Suez invasion of 1956, or Sir Anthony Nutting over Suez, did we not hound the Tories up and down the country for intolerance? Michael Foot referred to the 'Berias of Bournemouth'. If I ran into trouble for sticking to what was previously Party policy I could not really imagine the National Executive Committee of the Labour Party remaining totally indifferent to the damage this could do to the Party's reputation for tolerance. Those members of the N.E.C. who belonged to the Tribune Group had been foremost in proclaiming the right to dissent.

The second and overriding consideration was that the issue was too important to allow discretion to be the better part of valour. This was a point of view which my Lincoln opponents could never understand. Ralph Wadsworth, for instance, reproved me at a G.M.C. meeting on September 7th, 1971, not just for having been pro-Common-Market but for having been one of the public advocates of entry on TV and radio: 'There is a time to speak out and a time to keep quiet, and you should have realized that this was obviously an issue on which to keep quiet.' They thought I had gone out of my way deliberately to provoke them and that I must have done so for some unexplained reason of self-interest. But you go into politics to be more than a passive spectator of events. If you feel inhibited from speaking out on one of the most important issues of our time, there is no sense in being in politics at all. Political life becomes intolerable if you lose your self-respect.

In fact the crisis was postponed. To begin with, any idea that the negotiations for Britain's entry would be swift, simple and straightforward was soon dispelled. It seemed at the conference of the heads of states of the E.E.C. countries at The Hague in 1969 that Pompidou had removed the French veto. But for a long time after the negotiations were resumed, difficulties seemed to multiply rather than diminish. Only in May 1971 did French intentions become clear. The outstanding difficulties were then quickly resolved. Next, Harold Wilson proved very reluctant to come down on the anti-Common-Market side. Almost until the eve of the special Party Conference on the Common Market, held in the Central Hall, Westminster, on July 24th, he kept reassuring pro-Market colleagues that he would avoid a confrontation with them. Lastly, there were no indications from Lincoln that the G.M.C. would regard the Common Market issue as a test of Socialist credentials. I knew Pat Mulligan was against and that several other quite prominent left wingers were instinctively hostile to the whole concept of the Common Market. But, perhaps surprisingly, Leo Beckett and Ralph Wadsworth were not. They seemed at first impressed by my argument that we faced essentially a choice between closer ties with the United States or closer ties with the E.E.C. Domination by Americans was even less attractive to them than a close liaison with Frenchmen or Germans.

The first major row with my own Party officers after the 1970 election was in fact on a different issue, the Tory Industrial Relations Bill. This Bill had some features in common with the Labour Government's proposals contained in *In Place of Strife*. However, it went much farther in making industrial relations subject to control by the courts. The Bill was based on evidence given by the Conservative Lawyers' Association to the Royal Commission on Industrial Relations that Wilson had set up. The Conservative Government did not appear in the least deflated by the fact that this evidence had been rejected. To me much of the Bill seemed unlikely to promote better industrial relations; rather the reverse. As one employer in Lincoln put it to me later: 'If you have good relations with the employees you don't need the Bill. If you have bad ones it won't help.' On the other hand I could not regard it as a threat to the very existence of trade unions as some of its more extreme opponents claimed, especially those who had not read the Bill.

Early in January 1971, I accepted an invitation to speak on the Bill at a special meeting for shop stewards to be held in Grafton House, the Lincoln Party Headquarters. On the same platform there was to be Ernie Roberts, Assistant Secretary of the Amalgamated Union of Engineering Workers, whose political philosophy is that direct action by the workers is more effective than Parliamentary action by political parties and who favours political co-operation with Communists. When I arrived in the Party offices before the meeting, Beckett, Wadsworth, Mulligan and Don Gossop were there. Don Gossop was the new District Secretary of the A.U.E.W. who was to chair the meeting.

Don Gossop has not yet featured in this story and I should say a few words about him. He succeeded Ralph Wadsworth as Chairman of the Lincoln Labour Party and remained Chairman during several years of the 1966–70 Labour Government. He was also a Councillor and a prominent shop steward at G.E.C., working in the same research department as Leo Beckett. After Roy Lilley resigned as District Secretary of the Engineering Union in order to stand for its national executive committee, Don Gossop took his place. He was elected as the left-wing candidate, supported by Scanlon's wing of the Union.

In January 1973, the official Labour Party line, and that of the Trades Union Congress, was to oppose strike action against the Industrial Relations Bill. The A.U.E.W. refused to lay down a general line but left the decision to local districts. The Communist Party and the Trotskyites and other militant groups advocated strikes. So did Gossop and he was backed by the District Committee of the Engineering Union, the biggest union in Lincoln. However, the second biggest local union, the General and Municipal Workers (of which I was a member) opposed strike action and supported the line advocated by the T.U.C. I learnt that it was Gossop's intention, backed by the officers of the Lincoln Labour Party, to use the platform of this meeting to win general support for a strike.

I told them I was totally and utterly opposed to strike action. If a call for it was made from the platform I would attack it as strongly as I could. To strike on this issue would be undemocratic and unconstitutional. However much they disagreed with the Bill, industrial action was totally unjustified because the Government was carrying out policy which had been part of the election manifesto. Strike action would increase, not diminish, public sympathy for the Bill. More important, it was a method of protest that in the end could only lead to Fascism. Beckett, Wadsworth and Mulligan attacked me in turn, the first two bitterly and Mulligan more mildly, for showing a middle-class, legalistic and academic approach to politics. The life of the trade unions was at stake and there was no room for constitutional niceties. Gossop was more direct and warned me with some passion that if I took the line proposed, 'We will see that you are finished in Lincoln.' I refused to give way. In the end we agreed that if he did not raise the issue from the Chair and would do his best to prevent a motion being put from the floor, I would not refer to it in my speech.

By contrast the meeting that followed, attended by some one hundred and fifty to two hundred people, was rather quiet. I set out what the Bill was about and gave my comments on parts which I thought were bad and parts which were good. I said that overall it was a bad Bill. Ernie Roberts scarcely referred to the Bill but mainly attacked the Tory Government. As a whole the audience was surprisingly docile. I was questioned about my attitude to strike action and simply stated that I agreed with the Labour Party and T.U.C. view, which was against it. Support came from the N.U.G.M. Union Convener at the local G.E.C. works, Fred Tooley, the Chairman of the engineering branch.* He seemed unafraid of the wrath of the militants. No resolution was moved about strike action.

This meeting on the Industrial Relations Bill passed off without incident at the time. Soon afterwards I agreed to join the Lincoln Labour Party on the T.U.C. march against the Bill, from Hyde Park to Trafalgar Square. Having attacked uncon-

* Now Chairman of the Lincoln Democratic Labour Association.

stitutional forms of protest, the least I could do, I felt, was to support a peaceful protest march. But the row confirmed the feelings of the leaders of the Lincoln Labour Party that I did not see politics primarily as a class struggle. Increasingly they did.

A few months later the chances of avoiding a confrontation on the issue of the Common Market receded. Once Pompidou reached a clear understanding with Heath the outstanding problems seemed to disappear, as if with the wave of a magic wand. The very real problem of our financial contribution during the transitional period was solved on the basis of reasonable compromise, or so I thought. The solutions for the problems of New Zealand butter and Commonwealth sugar were acceptable to the countries affected, if not to their champions in the anti-Market camp or to those like Wilson who desperately needed an excuse for opposing the terms. The negotiations ended with a deal which George Thomson, Labour's Minister for Europe at the end of the Labour Government, said he would gladly have recommended to a Labour Cabinet and which, in his opinion, they would have accepted.

Ever since the second half of the 1950s I had strongly favoured Britain's entry into Europe. Now it looked almost certain of achievement. Nothing gives greater satisfaction in politics than seeing a major aim achieved, even if you have played no part in achieving it. On the other hand there would now be a question mark over my future as a Member of Parliament.

When Geoffrey Rippon came to the House of Commons on June 24th, 1971, to announce the final package, I saw no reason to keep silent and so I supported the terms. Ironically, the only other person who welcomed them from the Labour side that day was Sir Geoffrey de Freitas, my predecessor in Lincoln who had been back in the House since 1964 as M.P. for Kettering.

I cannot accuse Pat Mulligan, my Agent, of failing to warn me about what would happen. As soon as it was clear that terms for British entry would be agreed, in May 1971, I said I might have to resign as Front Bench spokesman for the Opposition. I explained that agreement with the European Community was now more likely than not and that I would probably feel bound to vote in favour of the terms agreed. He was horrified. Could I really contemplate voting with the Tories against a Three-Line Whip? I said that the Labour Party was entitled to change its mind about entry, which it looked like doing, but I could not be compelled to change mine. 'Then you will have to take the consequences,' he said, and it was quite clear what these would be.

I suggested an early meeting with the G.M.C. to discuss my differences and we provisionally fixed a Friday early in June. What I had not expected was that he would refuse to arrange a meeting of a kind I wanted. I envisaged a meeting between me, as the Member of Parliament, and the General Management Committee to discuss a problem between ourselves. As far as he was concerned, this was to be a meeting about the Party's attitude to the Common Market and, since I was in favour, he would not hold one without a prominent speaker against. As he failed to get Michael Foot or Eric Heffer for the date arranged, he cancelled this meeting and asked me to help get another speaker for July 2nd. There was no way of arranging the kind of meeting I would have liked. I therefore decided to ask the most reasonable of the confirmed anti-marketeers, John Silkin, a former Chief Whip in the Labour Government, who readily agreed to come. Much later one of the prominent members at Grafton House, Councillor Derek Miller, a deeply sincere left-winger, complained that I had never had a heart-to-heart talk with the G.M.C. members after the Market issue first came between us. The meeting which might have helped to clear the air never took place because my Agent foiled it. I should add that I rather doubt whether in the end it would have made much difference.

By Friday, July 2nd, the date for our debate, attitudes had crystallized. The G.M.C. was to consider resolutions on the following Monday for the official Labour Party Conference on July 17th. Ward meetings had already been held and anti-Market resolutions had already been passed at some of them. I did not realize this at the time. The meeting itself was open to all Party members and included members from the neighbouring constituencies of Gainsborough and Newark. It was the first time I became aware of a solid wall of opposition by the inner circle at Grafton House against our entry to Europe, almost irrespective of any terms. Beckett, the Chairman, was now passionately committed to fighting against entry. He gave us a little homily at the end of the meeting about accepting the decision of the Party nationally and locally whatever it might be. Wadsworth asked a hostile question; so—surprisingly—did Pat Mulligan. John Silkin himself acted as I had hoped. He was eloquent and hard-hitting in argument but also staunch in defence of tolerance, as indeed he had been as Chief Whip. He stated that when he was seeking support for a liberal regime of discipline to protect the left wing in the middle 1960s, he had much appreciated my support. It was not a comfortable meeting.

The resolution adopted by the G.M.C. the following Monday was even less comforting. It read:

'This Conference considers that there can be no benefit to the ordinary person for Britain, on entering the E.E.C.—quite the reverse—the cost of living would rise substantially and redundancies would follow the inevitable rationalization which would occur around the fringe areas of the Common Market wall.

'In consequence, Conference declares itself opposed to British entry and calls upon each member of the P.L.P. to do likewise.'

I cannot help feeling that the way had been carefully prepared for the passing of this resolution. It fitted very closely with Leo Beckett's closing remarks from the Chair at the end of the Silkin debate. He knew from Pat Mulligan that I would probably vote against a Three-Line Whip if one was imposed. I suspect the resolution was directed at me as much as at the Party Conference. Either it was a warning or it was designed to put me on the spot. The *Lincolnshire Echo* read the warning signs and prominently featured the threat to my future as Lincoln's M.P. Several letters were printed asking who the Grafton House lot (those who ruled at the Lincoln Labour Headquarters) thought they were.

When the special Labour Party Conference on the Common Market was held in July 1971 it went better than the pro-Marketeers had expected. The National Executive of the Labour Party had proposed that the conference should simply debate and take note. There was, however, a demand from the most determined anti-Marketeers that there should be a vote. We feared that this move would be successful and that a vote against the Tory terms would be passed. If so, the pressure at the Annual Conference in October would be to go farther, to reject entry altogether in principle and possibly to call for disciplinary action against M.P.s who failed to heed the views of the Conference. This after all had been called for implicitly by the Lincoln resolution.

Instead there was no vote. The pro-Europeans, notably John Mackintosh and George Thomson, spoke up effectively and received a surprising amount of applause. As the conference proceeded, the pro-Marketeers seemed to gain in confidence. Wilson's winding-up speech was the most anti-Market in tone that he had yet made and fell rather flat. It seemed as if he had misjudged the mood of the conference and had expected it to be much more overwhelmingly anti-Market. However, the National Executive Committee met shortly afterwards and laid down the official line that the Party would now campaign against entry in the terms negotiated, subject only to the vote of the Annual Conference.

After the special conference and particularly after the N.E.C. decision about the need for a propaganda campaign, the Officers of the Lincoln Labour Party seemed to become more confident that they could force me out. Although I saw no direct evidence of this at first (anyway August holidays followed shortly afterwards), it was reported to me by several of my friends and there was some retrospective confirmation from what happened in October. We had the curious situation that my constituency party were campaigning against the Market while I campaigned in favour. At a meeting organized by a local religious body, for example, they came along to heckle. They also organized a poll in the High Street, where anyone so minded could vote, and pointed to the 2–1 majority which it produced against entry as a sign of my lack of support.

On September 6th I met the General Management Committee at my request, not to discuss their attitude to the Market which I had to take as read, but to discuss the relations between a Member of Parliament and his constituency party and in particular that part of their resolution which called on M.P.s to vote in accordance with the decision of the party. I quoted Nye Bevan and Keir Hardie in favour of the view that M.P.s could not accept instructions from outside and must be regarded as representatives rather than delegates. Otherwise Parliament could not work. Anyway, surely no one would respect an M.P. who was a mere 'cabbage'. The meeting was very well attended, with about sixty to seventy people present, and what was most encouraging was the reappearance for the first time for many years of loyalists who used to defend the Labour Government against criticism from the left wing but who had ceased to play an active part in Lincoln Labour politics. Press reports made them feel that they should attend again because a crisis in my relations with the party was obviously imminent. Normally the G.M.C. would be attended by some thirty to forty people and the Left would have a majority of about 3 or 4 to 1, or even bigger. Now the balance looked more nearly even.

Despite a hostile speech from Ralph Wadsworth and one or two others and some sly digs from Leo Beckett in the Chair, who opened the meeting by referring to my membership of C.D.S. (long since disbanded), the meeting passed off reasonably well. The main arguments put against me, which were to become a familiar chorus later on, were, first, that the right to conscience which enabled M.P.s to abstain (and no more) applied to matters like Sunday Observance and abortion and questions of religion, but not to major policy decisions like the future of Britain; and, secondly, that one really could not disregard the majority view of both the local party and the full Labour Party Conference. At later meetings they could cite the majority view of the Parliamentary Labour Party as well.

The 1971 Annual Conference started in Brighton on Sunday,

October 4th. I ran across Leo Beckett that morning as I was on my way to chair a meeting of a group concerned with environmental questions. It was quite obvious that he had reached a stage of animosity beyond anything I had known before.

On Tuesday, October 6th, Conference voted against the Tory terms by 5 to 1. Given the certainty of a number of Conservative M.P.s voting against entry, delegates now sensed the possibility of defeating the Government when the vote came up in the House. The next day they were infuriated by reports in the press that a large number of Labour M.P.s were planning to vote for entry come what may, and were thus planning to disregard the Conference resolution. The anti-Market triumph of the Tuesday evening turned to ashes on the Wednesday morning. From my own point of view two developments were particularly ominous. First the press, particularly the *Guardian* and *The Times*, overstated my part in this 'betrayal'. Very sensibly, pro-Market Members of Parliament had during the previous four or five months built up a list of M.P.s who said they would vote for entry under any circumstances. Bill Rodgers kept the records and had acted as the Whip. Bill and I kept closely in touch and I knew more or less accurately who was intending to vote for entry, and who would abstain or vote against. However, the press suggested that I was the keeper of the list and one of the two main organizers. As the whipping later proved extremely efficient, I wish I deserved at least part of the credit for our success; but I cannot in all honesty claim that I did. I was a propagandist rather than an organizer. But the press reports were not calculated to soften the mood of my Lincoln opponents.

The second development was an item in the gossip column of *The Times* on October 7th. It stated that of M.P.s who would face difficulties with their local parties, I was the most obvious case.

> Pro-Market Labour M.P.s who are intending to vote for entry on October 28 are confidently expecting a little difficulty in their constituency parties. But Dick Taverne, one

> of their leading lights and a junior Minister at the Treasury between 1968–70, by general consent faces serious trouble in Lincoln . . .
>
> The signs are that the left and trade union delegates at Lincoln's general management committee will move a vote of no confidence in Taverne should he vote with the Government and there will subsequently be a powerful movement to prevent his readoption ...

Leo Beckett was quoted as saying: 'I personally hope that there would be a vote of no confidence in him if he votes in the Tory lobby.'

There was one other event of major importance before the vote in Parliament on October 28th. On the 18th, Granada TV asked me if I would appear in a *World in Action* programme about the constitutional position of a Member of Parliament vis-à-vis his party. Leo Beckett had already been approached and had told them that it would be for me to decide. I agreed. According to subsequent reports from the Granada team, when Leo heard of my agreement he gave the impression that he could not believe his luck.

I agreed because I thought that I would gain by bringing the argument before the largest possible audience. I believed that Burke's view of the duties of a Member of Parliament, namely that he should be a representative rather than a delegate, had popular support. People do not like to think that M.P.s are puppets voting as the local parties tell them. My impression was that even on the Common Market, where opinion polls showed the majority to be against entry, the public would feel it wrong for M.P.s to break their public commitments and repudiate their strongly held beliefs because their local party told them to toe the line.

If this estimate of public opinion was correct, then I felt the advantages of accepting Granada's invitation outweighed the disadvantages. The latter were obvious. To appear in a public wrangle with one's own Party Officers would provide ammunition to a future Conservative candidate in Lincoln. It would also damage the Party nationally. There were two big advantages: first, the more public the controversy became the more I would be able to count on the maximum turnout of friendly G.M.C. delegates at the critical meetings ahead. Secondly, it seemed a reasonable hope at the time that sooner or later public opinion could not be ignored by even the most diehard of my opponents.

The TV confrontation took everyone aback by its bitterness, myself included. It was a recorded programme. About half of it was to consist of interviews and half of a discussion between some G.M.C. members and myself. As one of the producers later told me, the latter part was so totally riveting that it was made the major part of the programme. Leo Beckett made a violent but very carefully prepared attack on me (he had notes in his hands) for my unbelievable arrogance in ignoring the views of the Conference and of the active Labour Party workers in my constituency. He also said in an interview that part of my trouble was my middle-class background: I was obviously ill at ease in the presence of mere foundry workers like himself. (In fact he is a foreman at G.E.C. in the Research Department.)

My own mail was very large and overwhelmingly favourable, but—more important—so were the letters to the local press. I noticed the impact of the programme that very evening, because I was in the middle of a meeting with shop stewards from the General and Municipal Workers Union in Lincoln. I dashed off in the middle of the meeting, as I had arranged to watch the programme at the house of some friends. When I returned to the meeting, it turned out that the shop stewards had managed to see it as well. The meeting had been about the Common Market. Before the programme, several members had been rather critical of my stand. Afterwards I had their full support. Fred Tooley, the Chairman of the local engineering union branch, was particularly angry at Leo Beckett's allegations that I could not talk to the working man. He complained that neither he nor his friends felt at ease in Leo Beckett's presence because of the extreme nature of his political views.

My opponents realized they had gone too far. The Party

Officers afterwards put in a complaint to Granada that the programme had been unfair in its allocation of time. This was because Leo Beckett and my critics had been given 70 per cent of the total time, whereas only about 20 per cent had been allotted to my friends and me. They had prepared a careful breakdown of the programme and they thought it showed clear evidence of bias in my favour (!). Since then the leading figures at Grafton House have felt that there is a plot by the media against them. Leo Beckett refused to appear on television again. Finally, it was an unusual television programme because it revealed a side of politics that is seldom seen. The Diarist of the *New Statesman* wrote on October 29th, 1971:

> Here at long last was politics in the raw—no kind of carefully-staged P.R. presentation but rather the authentic atmosphere of a G.M.C. that any local party activist would instantly recognize.

Three days after the broadcasting of the debate on television, Parliament voted on British entry into the Common Market. I dashed to Lincoln early that day to help in a local authority by-election. Pat Mulligan's last words to me before I caught the train back to London were: 'For God's sake abstain.' Earlier the Party Officers had been intransigent. Now I got the impression that they were looking for a compromise. With considerable regret I felt unable to meet them.

The vote itself was a famous victory. Bob Mellish, the Labour Chief Whip, had once told a deputation from the Labour Committee for Europe early in 1971 that there would be a Three-Line Whip against Britain's entry only over his dead body. Harold Wilson had assured some of his pro-Market colleagues earlier in the year that the worst that they could expect was a free vote but with a recommendation against entry from the Shadow Cabinet. But the Party Leader and his Chief Whip had changed their attitudes, not only about the merits of entry but also about the need for discipline. Heath announced at the last minute that there would be no Whip on the Government side. Wilson and Mellish would not follow suit. They opposed a motion requesting a free vote at a meeting of the Parliamentary Labour Party and it was defeated by 145 votes to 85. They were confident that the rebels would come into line. In the event 69 voted for entry and 20 abstained. The vital vote of principle for entry, on the basis of the arrangements made by the Government, was passed by 356 votes to 244.

5

DISMISSAL

The officers of the Lincoln Labour Party acted immediately, so quickly that their plans must have been carefully prepared. A meeting of the G.M.C. was due to be held on the following Monday, November 1st. Even if I had faced no crisis, I would have felt bound to attend in order to explain a vote against my Party on a matter of such importance. When I arrived I found that Leo Beckett and Pat Mulligan had two resolutions ready for immediate consideration by the G.M.C., both of them in similar terms. The first had been submitted by Ermine Ward (the ward of which Leo was a member) and the other came from a branch of the Engineering Union affiliated to the G.M.C. Number 5 Branch (which was Leo's trade union branch). They called for a vote of no confidence in me, and for my retirement at the next General Election as the Labour candidate. These resolutions could only have been passed on the previous Friday at the earliest, or on that very Monday at specially convened emergency meetings. None of the delegates or the local press had any knowledge of their terms, nor did any of the national papers, with one exception. This was the *Morning Star*, the Communist newspaper, which, as I found out later, carried full details of the resolution from the Engineering Union branch and stated that the motion would be moved against me that night.

At this stage Jim Cattermole, the Regional Organizer for the Labour Party in the East Midlands, pointed out to the Officers of the Party that to move the resolution as they were intending was contrary to the constitution of the Labour Party. He had to draw Pat Mulligan's attention to the requirement that in this kind of case two meetings of the G.M.C. were necessary: first a special meeting to consider whether a resolution calling for the retirement of the sitting Member of Parliament should be moved at all; if they voted that it should, then a second meeting was necessary after a delay of at least four weeks to vote on the actual question. He said that the motion of 'No confidence' could first be considered separately, but even for this the officers were bound to notify G.M.C. members on the Agenda for the meeting.

Nothing happened on November 1st except that a date for a consideration of the 'No confidence' motion was fixed. This was to be on November 16th.

The meeting on November 16th was tense but orderly; the arguments were by now familiar. So was my knowledge of those I could look to for support or opposition, but I was encouraged by the fact that supporters were far more numerous than had seemed possible only a few months before. There was one moment of light relief when Ralph Wadsworth was speaking and so angered one of my supporters, known as 'Big Barry', that the latter stood up and shouted, 'I'll knock your bloody block off!'

The line of argument put forward by my critics was carefully designed to win the maximum support among the large number of trade union delegates. It was based entirely on loyalty; the need to accept Three-Line Whips and majority decisions, especially Conference decisions, and the immorality of voting with the Tories. They acknowledged that I had been a good constituency M.P. and that I had made a useful contribution to the Labour Party. In the circumstances, however, it was best for me to look for another seat.

There was a strong streak of hypocrisy in these arguments. Those who now called for the acceptance of Conference decisions had themselves never accepted decisions not to their liking. In 1961, after the Labour Party Conference decision rejecting neutralism and unilateral nuclear disarmament, they had continued to campaign strenuously in favour of both. I also pointed out that I had voted against a Three-Line Whip on one occasion only (when there was a free vote on the Conservative side), whereas Michael Foot and the other leading figures of the

Tribune Group had voted against Three-Line Whips regularly. In 1968 they voted in the same lobby as the Conservatives and thereby endangered the survival of the Labour Government at the time. The bland answer was that the individuals in question did not represent Lincoln and their case was not being considered.

Undoubtedly there were some loyal trade unionists who agreed strongly with their general line. They regarded it as axiomatic that majority decisions must be accepted. They could not conceive that anyone should actually vote in the same lobby as Conservatives. They bitterly resent my rebellion, and that of the other sixty-eight, and have not forgiven it to this day.

The actual vote on the resolution against me was adverse, but close: 55 in favour and 51 against, with five abstentions. It seemed at the time quite a good result for me. I think Beckett & Co. were surprised at the narrow margin of the figures.

In the fourteen days after this vote, for the first time since my adoption as Labour Candidate, there seemed a reasonable prospect of my supporters gaining control of the G.M.C. We were swept along by an optimism which proved unjustified.

I was invited to a meeting of the largest of the affiliated branches of the Engineering Union, Number 6, where the same motion was being debated that had already been passed by Number 5 Branch. It was a call for a vote of no confidence and for my compulsory retirement at the next election. Despite strong opposition from one of the councillors who had already voted against me in his Ward, but saw nothing wrong in exercising his right to vote a second time in the union branch, the motion was rejected by more than 2 to 1. (Under the Labour Party constitution it is permissible for a person to vote twice. He can vote in his capacity as a Ward member as well as in his union.) This seemed a useful victory, as the meeting then instructed its six delegates to vote for me at subsequent meetings of the G.M.C. However, in the event, the delegates of this branch, with one exception, disregarded their instructions and continued to vote against me. They were friends of Beckett's.

The second favourable development was that soon after my

vote against the Three-Line Whip, I was re-elected unopposed as Chairman of the Parliamentary Labour Party's Economic and Finance Group. I was also reappointed by Harold Wilson as official Economic Spokesman, second to Roy Jenkins. I was not especially eager to be appointed to either post. My own preference would in some ways have been for the relative freedom of the Back Benches. However, Roy Jenkins wanted me to be his deputy and had argued strongly and successfully with Wilson that I should be reappointed. What is more, I felt both appointments were likely to help me in Lincoln because they showed that the Parliamentary Party and even the Leader of the Party took a different view of my act of rebellion from my local party.

I also called a meeting of friendly G.M.C. delegates, representing each of the Wards, to consider tactics. The night before, the Lincoln Party's Executive Committee had decided to recommend to the G.M.C. that for the time being no further action should be taken on the motion for my retirement. It was a clear sign that my opponents were now in retreat. We decided not to accept this truce but to force a vote that the whole issue of my retirement should be dropped rather than suspended. Representatives from each Ward also undertook to canvass their friends to attend the next annual meetings of the Wards, to vote in new delegates and change the composition of the G.M.C. in my favour by the next Annual General Meeting in March.

However, the counter-revolution failed. Most of my friends were not dedicated political warriors like those on the other side. Some of them had too many other commitments and did not always manage to be there on the vital day, whether at G.M.C. meetings or at the annual meetings of their ward. Even if they were there themselves, they did not find the time to ensure the attendance of others with like views. Moderation of political views and exclusive dedication to politics seldom go hand in hand. To reject extremism in politics is also to reject the view that involvement in politics matters more than anything else. To Marxists and others on the far Left, twenty-four-hours-a-day politics comes naturally. They have more stamina and determination.*

When the next meeting of the G.M.C. was held on December 6th we reached a stalemate. The officers of the party had not expected a vote and had not whipped up their supporters to be present in full strength. When a vote seemed imminent, my opponents prolonged the debate and some of them made frantic telephone calls to summon absent supporters. On our side several key members were ill or absent for other reasons. A motion that the Executive Committee's proposal for no further action for the time being should be referred back with a recommendation against any further action at all was finally put to the vote. It ended in a tie: 45 to 45. The Chairman therefore ruled that it was not carried. The G.M.C. was not only divided in numbers: by now it was divided geographically with the two sides sitting on opposite sides of the room in Grafton House rather like Government and Opposition in Parliament.

At the height of this stalemate the time seemed ripe for compromise. I had already indicated that I was willing to accept the Whip on the detailed legislation now required by our entry into Europe, unless the issue of principle was raised. My opponents argued that I was being inconsistent. I must admit this was right, and in retrospect I regret it. But this concession had already mollified a few of my opponents in Lincoln.

We now arranged a meeting for the officers and myself to discuss where we stood. I wanted to see whether there was any way in which we could come to a working relationship. The Officers made it clear that no such relationship was possible. Ralph Wadsworth acted as their spokesman and took the line that since the G.M.C. was now deadlocked, the only way out was for me to retire voluntarily and look for another seat. I learned that fifty G.M.C. members had without the knowledge of their colleagues signed a petition to Transport House in which they acknowledged my past services to Lincoln and the Party but requested that in the light of my vote for entry to the

* I have since found that such dedication is not confined to the left-wing. Many members of the Lincoln Democratic Labour Association seem equally dedicated.

Community and their own strong feelings against entry, Transport House should find me another seat. I am not sure whether this was naivety on their part or a tactical move to appear conciliatory. Several of them certainly knew that candidates cannot be forced on constituencies. I declined the offer to retire.

When the annual meetings of the wards took place, instead of my strengthening my support on the G.M.C. the balance was shifted firmly back against me. Beckett and his friends organized much better than mine. They brought their supporters to the ward meetings in cars as if they were ferrying voters to the polling booths in a local election. Additional union representatives were affiliated to the G.M.C. In the doubtful wards some of our key people failed to get elected to the G.M.C. One of my friends warned me afterwards that, 'Heavy artillery is being moved up to the front line. It does not look too good.'

At the Annual General Meeting of the new G.M.C. in March 1972 nearly all of the new Executive and all of the new officers were hard-line opponents. The *Lincolnshire Echo* reported the re-election of Leo Beckett and other determined left-wingers to the key posts and suggested that the signs were ominous for my survival. It was right. I knew that one further step out of line would almost certainly mean compulsory retirement for me.

By now I was quite prepared for a new showdown even if this would mean defeat. I had worked out all the possible consequences and did not necessarily find them unattractive. Relations with the officers had become impossible and were clearly past repair. I could not pretend that we could work amicably together; I could hardly drink with them in the Labour Club without a hypocrisy of which I felt incapable. I felt that the situation would have to be resolved either by winning an appeal to the National Executive Committee of the Labour Party against a decision that I should retire, or by standing as an Independent in a by-election. I realized that the latter course would mean a break, possibly a permanent break, with the Labour Party. However, by February of 1972 even this was no longer unthinkable. I could not see how the Tribune Left could be dislodged from their control of Party Conference, or prevented from extending their control over the National Executive Committee. Even in Parliament the Party was passing into the hands of the left wing. Opposition to our entry into the European Community was gradually sliding into opposition on principle, not just on the terms of entry. With Michael Foot and Peter Shore as our Front Bench spokesmen on Community affairs it could hardly be otherwise. I anticipated that we should be soon committed to a policy of withdrawal, or at the best of a renegotiation on impossible terms. I was longing to resign as Front Bench spokesman, so that I could abstain on the European Communities Bill then passing through Parliament, and was in fact restrained from doing so only because it would gravely embarrass my pro-Market colleagues. I had told Roy Jenkins that in my view all the pro-Community spokesmen should resign, or at least those who felt sufficiently strongly; but personally he was not yet willing to take this step.

On April 17th I resigned as Front Bench spokesman because of the Shadow Cabinet's proposal to support a motion for a referendum. Just before Easter Wilson had once again changed his mind. Earlier he had declared on television that he would never support a referendum under any circumstances and it was official Party policy to oppose one. A motion calling for a referendum if a General Election before entry to the Common Market was refused, had been voted down at the last Party conference by a 2 to 1 majority. Nevertheless, on Anthony Wedgwood Benn's prompting, the Shadow Cabinet proposed to support a Conservative motion, moved by Neil Marten and backed by Enoch Powell, that a referendum must be held. With full Labour support the motion was likely to be carried.

Not only was I opposed to a referendum, but it seemed to me a good issue on which to make a stand against the steady slide of the Labour Party into a posture of total opposition to entry into the Community.

When we left for our Easter holiday in Wales, I felt deeply depressed at the attitude of most of my pro-Market colleagues. Many of them had been at a party given by Bob Maclennan,

M.P., and his wife on the eve of our holiday and only George Thomson thought it an issue worth a major conflict.

When we returned from our holiday on Sunday, April 15th, I learned that Roy Jenkins, George Thomson and Harold Lever were going to resign from the Shadow Cabinet, which they did next day. I felt enormously relieved.

Ralph Wadsworth later criticized the timing of all the resignations. My crime of voting against a Three-Line Whip on October 28th had been aggravated by the fact that I did so on the day of a local by-election. Now I had chosen to resign, deliberately he felt, in the middle of the annual municipal election campaign. It seemed we had our priorities wrong about the relative importance of national and local affairs.

What followed was inevitable. Their confidence increased by local election results which were better than they expected, the officers of the Lincoln Party arranged a special meeting of the G.M.C., as required by the Party constitution, to vote on the motion whether a resolution for my retirement should be considered at a further meeting. The first meeting was held on May 10th and the motion was passed by 55 votes to 38. It was a relatively short affair with both sides keeping back their main arguments for the later debate. Apart from the mover and the seconder of the resolution, only my own supporters spoke. The second meeting required by the Party constitution was fixed for June 16th.

From a breakdown of the names of all accredited G.M.C. delegates it was clear that a majority would be against me. Theoretically about a hundred and fifty-five could attend. The maximum strength of our supporters was about seventy, but some of these were ill. Others were due to go away on holiday or were not entirely immune to pressure from the Officers. Forty-five to fifty-five was a more realistic estimate of our total strength. Our only hope was to persuade the wards at meetings before the final vote to mandate their delegates to vote in my favour. If such meetings did not take place, or if Party members were not given proper notice, I thought it would give me a powerful case on appeal to the National Executive Committee on the grounds that individual members would have been given no chance to express their views about my dismissal.

Several developments before June 16th deserve mention, as they throw some light on the way a determined left-wing group in the Labour Party is prepared to act to achieve its ends.

First, the pressure on Councillors was considerable. One Councillor, who was originally one of my supporters, refused to vote for me at an earlier meeting on a show of hands. His neighbour asked him why. 'They will see me,' he said. When a secret ballot was then ordered he said, 'That's all right, now I can vote for Dick.' He had originally appealed to me to hold a supporters' meeting, 'as they will act against us next', but had then decided it would be safer if he did not personally attend. After the local elections three Councillors who were chairmen of Council Committees were deprived of their chairmanships.* No explanation was given. After inquiries the *Echo* published a prominent report that they had been sacked because they were my supporters. They had interviewed the Councillors concerned and obtained statements. At the next meeting of the Labour Group on the Council, the Agent, Pat Mulligan, not himself a Councillor, formally moved a vote of censure on the three for speaking to the press. (The policy of Labour Councillors was always decided beforehand by a meeting of the Group at which some non-councillors could attend and help determine the policy, which had to be strictly complied with.)

Next there was, to put it negatively, no attempt to give ordinary Party members any say in my dismissal. Where ward meetings were held, notices of the meeting went to only a small fraction of the total ward membership. In no case did the Agenda show that my case was to come up for discussion. Pat Mulligan admitted at the later hearing before the Committee of Inquiry set up by the National Executive, that special notice was usually given when wards were to consider nominations for the panel of Council candidates. It was not done for meetings

* Two of these are now Democratic Labour Councillors; the third was the only Labour Councillor to survive in the District Council elections of June 1973!

to consider the future of the Member of Parliament. Again, some wards never met at all. The chairmen of two wards, both of whom were my supporters, asked for meetings to be held, but their requests were refused. One was blocked by the Secretary of the ward, who was one of my opponents. The other was told by Pat Mulligan that a chairman had no power to call a meeting.

In one ward the Chairman, an officer of the Party, found strong opposition. First he tried to stop a discussion of my case. Members insisted on discussing it. Then he refused to allow a vote. He also refused to allow the ward delegates to express any views, because, he said, they had to make up their own minds at the G.M.C. It would be wrong to seek to limit their discretion or to influence their judgment. (The basic case against me, of course, was that I had not obeyed the mandate of my G.M.C. to vote as they directed but had used my own discretion on the merits of the issue.)

Long before June 16th I knew about the irregularities. I felt I had enough grounds for appeal to the N.E.C. if I decided to appeal at all, and I knew that if I wanted to stay as a Labour candidate I would have to appeal. All I hoped for from the final meeting was the closest possible vote to help with my next steps.

I had, in the meantime, arranged for an opinion poll. It was vital that the poll should be independently conducted. Accordingly I asked Professor Anthony King of Essex University if he could arrange for such a poll and he referred me to Richard Jay, a lecturer in the Department of Politics. I submitted two questions which Richard Jay agreed were fair and not biased. The first read as follows:

> Dick Taverne has publicly expressed strong support for entry into the Common Market. His Party, locally and nationally, are opposed to entry on present terms. Do you think he was right to vote in accordance with his views or should he have voted with his Party?

Three boxes were provided for ticks to say: Right—Wrong—Don't know. The second question was:

Do you approve or disapprove of Dick Taverne as your M.P.?

The poll was a postal poll and postcards were sent to eight hundred electors chosen by Richard Jay from a random sample from the Electoral Register. After a week a reminder was sent to the same addressees. As the reminder gave a second opportunity to record a vote to anyone who had lost his card, the votes on the reminder slips and on the original cards were counted separately in case they showed a different pattern. In the event, they did not.

The results were very favourable. Over 75 per cent replied. On the question of my vote 71 per cent said I was right, 21 per cent said that I was wrong. On the second question 79 per cent approved of me as their Member of Parliament and 12 per cent disapproved. The result of the poll was announced a few days before the G.M.C. meeting that was to take the decisive vote.

Nothing unexpected happened at this meeting, which was held on June 16th, 1972. The arguments, already fully rehearsed, were a formality. As soon as the list of names of delegates had been read out and checked, I mentioned to the Regional Officer that by my reckoning there were 44 definitely in my favour and 70 definitely against, with 11 uncertain whom I would expect to break evenly. The vote was 75 to 50 in favour of my retirement. Pat Mulligan was by now so involved that he actually cast a vote himself, even though he was not a delegate, and his vote had to be retrieved on the instructions of the Regional Officer.

The obvious question, which many people asked, is why this happened to me in Lincoln. There were sixty-nine Labour M.P.s who voted for entry on October 28th, 1971. Only one other Member of Parliament had to face a call for his retirement, Edward Lyons, in West Bradford. He won the vital vote by 35 to 20.

It has been argued and widely assumed that any Member of Parliament in trouble with his own party has only himself to blame and that like my rebel colleagues I should have been able to avoid a confrontation. I have no doubt that to some extent this is true. I cannot truthfully claim that my difficulties were solely due to a left-wing plot, or to a stand on principle, with no fault on my side. There must be few divorces in which one partner is wholly to blame.

Some of my opponents later explained that I did not spend enough time 'drinking with the lads' and tended to take Party workers for granted. This is probably fair criticism. I always regarded constituency cases and meetings with various constituency organizations as a top priority. As a result my reputation as a constituency Member was good—at a poll taken by the Opinion Research Centre on October 7th, 1972, 82 per cent thought I was a good Member of Parliament and only 2 per cent thought I was a bad one. (I suspect a slight myth has grown up about quite how good I was.) But my contacts with some of the active workers should probably have been more regular. I saw my main critics often enough. But I might have spent more time with their followers, those whom they converted. I feel now in retrospect that I might have made a more determined effort to keep on good terms with the people whose views I profoundly disagreed with. Again, although I spent at least forty to fifty days a year on average in my constituency, I always made a special effort to keep Saturday nights and Sundays for my family. This I certainly do not regret. Nevertheless, as the critical situation first developed in the 1966–70 period, it would have been wiser from a political point of view to have spent a larger part of the weekend 'with the lads'.

Next, I must confess I enjoy an argument. Had I been wiser I should perhaps have avoided one at times when I hated to see statements which I thought misleading or inaccurate go unchallenged. There were, in fact, many occasions when, for the sake of peace, I kept quiet. On the other hand, Leo Beckett once told me in 1970 at a Labour Party Conference, when he had complained about Wilson's double talk, that the reason they liked me despite our disagreements was because they knew where I stood.

What I do not accept (perhaps it is hardly to be expected that

I should) is a statement which has been frequently repeated, and which can in each case be traced back to one remark in the Granada *World in Action* programme on October 25th, that I am ill at ease with the working man and the trade unionist. I was often ill at ease with Leo Beckett, who made the original remark, especially when our political differences were at their greatest. I had the uncomfortable feeling that what I said would later be used as evidence against me. It often was. Others with impeccable working-class backgrounds felt equally ill at ease with him if they did not share his views. Most of those who left the Party with me after the final breach, and became the mainstay of my by-election Committee, are solidly working-class and trade unionist. I do not believe any of us are inhibited by class barriers.

One alternative strategy would have been to organize the loyalists at a much earlier stage, during the early years of the Labour Government, before the balance in the G.M.C. had swung almost irretrievably to the Left. It would have required spending many days in Party manœuvres, probably at the expense of pursuing constituency problems. I am not sure that it would have succeeded. First, there was the difficulty I have already referred to, that moderates are seldom full-time politicians. Before 1967 when there was no apparent crisis, I could not have mobilized support because there was no obvious need. When the attacks by the Left on the Labour Government started in earnest, many of the loyalists had not much stomach for active politics because they too had been affected by the general disillusionment.

It is worth recording how Leo Beckett and his allies established influence. By 1967 the Labour Party had modern club premises in Lincoln, with a bar serving snacks, in the same building as the office. Leo and the other officers would be there at lunchtime and in the evening. He and his family seemed to live there. Any club member who expressed any interest in politics would be given the most assiduous attention. Eager Party members would be told that they might be needed as a ward Secretary or even as a potential candidate for the Council.

At the same time they would hear Leo's views on Socialism and the not dissimilar views of others like Ralph Wadsworth, Don Gossop or Pat Mulligan. Even if Leo and his friends had been less persuasive, it would have been hard to resist the perks, like becoming a Councillor or the distinction of being treated as one of the inner circle, which expressions of similar views could bring. The same kind of tactics are used by the Tribune Group at Annual Party Conferences. I do not condemn them. They are a perfectly legitimate way of proselytizing. They do, however, help to explain why activists wield influence out of all proportion to their numbers. By their perpetual presence in Grafton House the leading figures of the Lincoln Labour Party lost contact with opinion outside Grafton House and failed to realize their increasing unpopularity; but it gave them an almost unshakeable hold over the Party machine.

How left-wing were the leading figures of the Lincoln Labour Party? On the whole they were neither Communist nor anti-Communist; though some of them were distinctly less anti-Communist than others. One Vice-Chairman who held office during the latter part of the Labour Government argued in 1968 at one G.M.C. meeting that one of the many and most serious crimes of the Labour Government was its refusal to advertise in the *Morning Star*. He regarded this as the only socialist newspaper. Several G.M.C. members supported him.

One person who was the constant companion of the Party leaders in the middle 'sixties disappeared from Grafton House only to emerge later as the Secretary of the local Communist Party. He was a quiet character whom I never heard express any political views at all.

A regular visitor to Lincoln and Grafton House was Ernie Roberts, the Assistant General Secretary of the Engineering Union. He seemed on very close terms with Leo Beckett and Pat Mulligan. They must have known that he had been refused endorsement as a Labour candidate by the Labour Party's National Executive Committee (before it was dominated by the left wing) because of the nature of his views. At the last May Day rally I attended, in 1972, Pat Mulligan and Leo

Beckett asked two Young Socialists sitting by the door to sell a pamphlet written by Ernie Roberts about unemployment. It was a pamphlet published by the Institute for Workers' Control. I read it during the meeting and found it very hard to believe that it was written by someone who could be a member of the Labour Party. It praised the attacks made on Sir Stafford Cripps during the period of the first Labour Government by Pritt, who was a staunch defender of the Communists and had been expelled from the Labour Party for his Communist views in the late 1940s. It echoed the call by the Communist Secretary of the Second International for direct action and factory occupation as the best road to socialism. Its main theme was that industrial action was far more effective than Parliamentary action. It ended with a call for all workers—Communist, Catholic and Labour alike—to unite in the parties for the fight against capitalism. The whole meeting was used as a rally to raise support locally for Ernie Roberts's unsuccessful election campaign against Jim Conway for the General Secretaryship of the Amalgamated Union of Engineering Workers.

As already stated, when immediately after my vote on October 28th, 1971, a resolution was rushed through one of the branches affiliated to the G.M.C. from the Engineering Union, the *Morning Star* was informed but no other newspaper. I cannot believe that Leo Beckett, who moved the resolution at the Branch, had no hand in telling the Press.

Finally, Don Gossop, a former Chairman of the Party and now District Secretary of the Engineering Union, was elected on the left-wing Scanlon ticket; in return he used his influence on behalf of the candidature for the Executive Committee of his union of Dixon, a Communist Party member, standing against a loyal member of the Labour Party. He was criticized by his union colleagues for using his official position as District Secretary for this purpose.

Apart from their refusal to regard the Communist Party as an undesirable ally in some cases, there were strong links between officers of the Lincoln Party and the Institute for Workers' Control at Nottingham. This is run by Ken Coates, who was for a time expelled from the Labour Party because of his views, but was later readmitted as a member. Leo Beckett and Pat Mulligan went to the Institute for weekend schools in 1971. There is no constitutional reason why they should not have gone. The Institute is not a body proscribed by the Labour Party. No one, however, can deny that the Institute belongs to the far Left of the Party. Ernie Roberts is a regular contributor; its general philosophy favours class revolution, direct action in industry, strikes for political ends, and seems impatient of the parliamentary approach. It has much more in common with Trotskyism than with social democracy.

Lastly, the officers of the Labour Party made no objections to the presence on the General Management Committee of one very active member who used Grafton House for the distribution of the *Workers' Press*, who distributed literature calling for young people to join the Trotskyists as opposed to the Labour Party, and who took pictures of our final G.M.C. meetings for the *Workers' Press* as its local representative.

I do not contend that Leo Becket and Pat Mulligan, or for that matter Don Gossop or Ralph Wadsworth, did not feel loyalty to the Labour Party. It was, however, a totally different Labour Party which they sought to establish than the one for which I suspect most people vote. They belonged to the left wing of the Tribune Group. They were in regular touch with leading Tribune figures such as Mikardo and Norman Atkinson. To visiting speakers they boasted of their proud record of unrelenting militancy as a local party.

At least some of my difficulties were therefore due to the seeming inevitability of a conflict between a former officer of the C.D.S. and the very left-wing officers at Grafton House.

6

BY-ELECTION

At first I was not sure that I wanted to appeal to the National Executive Committee. Because my opponents had neglected or refused to allow the ordinary Party members a say, I felt I had good grounds for such an appeal, although this did not mean that it might not fail for political reasons. Recently the person who appeared the stronger of two candidates for the post of General Secretary of the Labour Party, Gwyn Morgan, had been defeated by the weaker candidate, Ron Hayward, almost entirely because of the latter's support for the Tribune line. (This was not a conversion of long standing. In the C.D.S. days, Ron Hayward seemed friendly to our campaign.) Roy Jenkins had warned me that it was doubtful if anyone who had voted against Gwyn Morgan would vote to uphold my case.

I was tempted to resign at once and fight a by-election as an Independent, on the grounds that even if I did win an appeal my position with the local party would be impossible. Very few of my friends favoured this course. The person who finally persuaded me against it was George Brown. I visited him two nights after the vote. He urged most strongly and powerfully that whatever my eventual intentions, I first had to fight my fight within the Party. I had to show such strength in Lincoln that the National Executive Committee would not dare to refuse my appeal. We should organize a large public meeting, the biggest public meeting ever held in Lincoln, at which Taverne talked to his town. George was willing to speak himself if I wanted him.

The prospects for this policy seemed enhanced the next morning when I was informed by the *Lincolnshire Chronicle*, the local weekly paper, that they had carried out an opinion survey in

Labour areas which showed if anything even stronger support than the poll carried out by Richard Jay.

However, the National Executive Committee of the Labour Party upset my plans. My case was first to be considered by its Organization Sub-Committee. This met on July 17th and rejected a move by the Labour Party's National Chairman, Anthony Wedgwood Benn, to dispose of the appeal at once without a hearing. It decided instead that a Committee of Inquiry consisting of John Chalmers from the Boilermakers' Union, Jim Diamond from the Steelworkers' and Tom Bradley, M.P., should interview the Lincoln officers and myself on July 24th. The Organization Sub-Committee would then consider its Inquiry report on July 25th and the full National Executive Committee would reach a final decision on the 26th. The appeal was therefore to be swiftly concluded. (My friends on the N.E.C. had expected that the appeal would be spread out over several months.) In itself there was nothing objectionable about this timetable. However, I was asked in a letter from Ron Hayward not to engage meantime in any activities which might prejudice the deliberations of the N.E.C.

My friends begged me to cancel my proposed meeting. It would be an act of defiance against the N.E.C.; it would turn against me one or two who might otherwise support my appeal. In the end I yielded, with the greatest reluctance, on the grounds that if I was seeking to persuade the National Executive Committee to help me I could hardly ignore its requests.

My Lincoln friends, whose opinion I valued greatly, said that the decision must be my own in the light of circumstances which only I could properly assess.

There is no need to elaborate here the arguments I advanced before the Committee of Inquiry. I reproduce the case on which they were based in Appendix A. Mainly I relied on the failure of the Lincoln Labour Party to consult their members, which was, I felt, a breach of a requirement clearly implied in the constitution. Pat Mulligan who put the local party's case was certainly unable to answer the detailed evidence I was able to present about meetings not held, or of which no proper notification was given. The Committee seemed impressed, and judging their reactions as a lawyer assesses the mood of the Court, I came away convinced that my chances of a successful appeal looked favourable. (I had mixed feelings about this, as the prospect of a by-election looked increasingly attractive. When asked by Roy Hattersley immediately afterwards how the hearing had gone, I replied, truthfully, 'I'm afraid it went very well.')

The next night I knew that I had lost. I heard that the Committee of Inquiry had in fact recommended that my appeal should be upheld, and had done so unanimously. They had found that there had been a breach of natural justice and a failure to consult ordinary Party members. But the Organization Sub-Committee only upheld the recommendation of the Committee of Inquiry by the casting vote of the Chairman, John Chalmers. Apparently Ian Mikardo (a great friend of the Lincoln Labour Party leaders) had stated at once that he would not accept the Committee's report. If the National Executive Committee did so, constituency parties would think it was a fiddle. Anthony Wedgwood Benn supported him strongly, introducing his remarks by stating that this was nothing personal; after all he had been a close personal friend of mine for over twenty years. (I had not realized that he had these strong feelings of friendship. I had seen quite a lot of him before I entered Parliament but had not really had much contact with him for the last ten years.*) Although I had just won the vote, it was clear that the left-wingers on the National Executive Committee were determined to find against me whatever the Inquiry had recommended. As the left wing had a majority on the N.E.C. there could be no possible chance of winning at next day's hearing of the full Committee.

My parliamentary friends, who had reached the same conclusion, asked me about my intentions. I confirmed that I would fight a by-election. They pressed me not to. I was given a lift home that night by Bob Maclennan, the Labour M.P. for

* At the 1973 Party Conference Benn attributed my victory in Lincoln to 'Stalinism' in the local party.

Caithness and Sutherland. He perhaps came nearest of anyone to shaking my determination, with his quiet but forceful arguments. He urged that if I did as I proposed I could never under any circumstances return to the Labour Party; nor would the Party ever split. It would surely be better to accept my fate and retire gracefully at the next General Election. I could then make a comeback when, as must surely one day happen, the Labour Party returned to sanity and the quarrels over the Common Market were only a distant memory. It might not be a very appealing scenario, but it was the only hope.

The next day, the National Executive Committee dismissed my appeal by 12 votes to 8. From the accounts I received it appeared that numbers at first seemed fairly even. Benn, however, in the Chair, dealt with other matters first and discussion of my case started only towards the end of the morning. By the time the vote was taken, which was nearly two o'clock, some of those who might have voted for me had left. Callaghan had another engagement (with the Russian Ambassador). Jim Diamond had made a strong speech in my favour but had then left to see some of his steelworkers ('Far more important than any M.P.,' he had said). Wilson had thought it diplomatic not to attend at all. I am told that, apart from Jim Diamond, others who spoke for me were Tom Bradley, Denis Healey, Shirley Williams and Ted Short. I was particularly grateful to Fred Mulley, who stayed to the final vote despite a most pressing engagement which he was forced to miss. Benn later explained to a meeting of the P.L.P. why the views of the Committee of Inquiry and the Organization Sub-Committee had been overruled: 'Although there was a breach of natural justice, there had been no breach of the Party constitution.'

There followed an uncomfortable period of waiting before I announced my decision to resign. I could not announce it at once, as I had first to discuss the matter with my Lincoln supporters. Further, I intended to take a good holiday first. What was in a way touching, but at the same time deeply embarrassing, was the weight of sympathy and condolence I received. I was unable to explain that sympathy was misplaced. As far as I was concerned the fight was only just about to start and it was much too early to write my political obituary.

The reactions of my supporters in Lincoln certainly gave me every encouragement. A committee of about twenty people had been formed before the final vote of the G.M.C. with Fred Tooley, a leading member of the General and Municipal Workers' Union, as Chairman, Councillor Fred Allen as Vice-Chairman (he was one of those displaced from his chairmanship of a Council Committee because of his support for me), Ken Rawding as Treasurer and Joe Ghose, a young insurance representative who had been President of the Junior Chamber of Commerce, as Secretary. All of them were Labour Party members.

I told the Committee about my feelings that I wanted to fight a by-election as an Independent. Now it was one thing for them to support me in my fight inside the Party; to support me as an Independent was a different proposition. They could face expulsion from the Party. Many of them had spent their lives in the Labour Party, canvassing, attending the G.M.C., lending their homes as committee rooms during elections. These were the loyalists who had stood by the Labour Government in the days of its greatest unpopularity, unlike the leading figures at Grafton House who had been the Labour Government's chief critics. The emotional wrench would be great. I warned them of the seriousness of any decision on their part to come with me.

All but two said they would continue to support me. Most of them felt that Grafton House could no longer command their loyalty. Many of them were as disillusioned with the behaviour of the Labour Party, nationally as well as locally, as I was. In fact I got the impression that they greeted my decision with relief because it meant that they did not have to accept the victory of the left wing in Lincoln.

They were sure we would win. But we agreed that I could not call myself Independent—as indeed I had no intention of doing—as this had always been equivalent to being a Conservative in Lincoln. Preferably I should keep the word 'Labour' in my title. After all, none of us had changed our views since the last election. We settled on the description 'Democratic Labour' to emphasize the undemocratic nature of Grafton House and of the method of my dismissal. Personally I would have preferred to call myself 'Social Democrat' but this is not, or not yet at any rate, a familiar term to most voters. For Lincoln, in my special situation, Democratic Labour seemed right.

I should also mention that very few of them, though there were some exceptions, were contemplating a new alignment of the Left. Their main hopes were that if I won at the by-election and the General Election, the demoralization at Grafton House would be so great that our friends could recapture control of the local party and invite me back to be the official Labour candidate. As I had rather suspected, in the course of time and in the heat of the campaign attitudes to the Labour Party altered, and more and more of them came to think of the possibilities of starting something new if left-wing domination of the Labour Party should continue.

Soon after the decision of the National Executive Committee I attended a meeting with some of my parliamentary friends. Their reaction was completely different. They were almost unanimously against my resigning to force a by-election. They were sure my career would be ruined. In the first place all except Roy Jenkins thought I would lose the by-election. But even if I won, no one could see any political future for me. They were all agreed that there was no support for the idea of a new social democratic party. Moreover there was a certain coolness in their attitude towards me because they felt that my suicidal foolhardiness would weaken the influence of the Jenkinsites, since I had always been associated with them within the Party. All of them would be tainted by my disloyalty. Their mood and assessment was reflected in an article about me written soon afterwards by David Watt of the *Financial Times*, whom I have always regarded as one of the ablest of political commentators, which expressed sympathy for me personally, correctly anticipated my future actions and diagnosed that these would damage the fortunes of my friends. He had clearly talked to some of them.

I made it quite clear to them that my own mind was made up and that I was unlikely to change it. I did, however, take note of their views about timing and tactics. My original intention was to resign shortly after the summer holidays, some time in the middle of September. I wanted to be certain that my decision was public before the Lincoln Labour Party set into motion the procedure for the selection of a new candidate which they were planning to do at once. As soon as this occurred, some of the wards would be likely to nominate me; I would then fail to be short-listed and, if short-listed, I would certainly fail to be selected by the G.M.C. Several people asked me afterwards why I did not offer myself for reselection. It was a somewhat naive view that those who had sacked me would be ready to select me again. If I waited until after my selection had been turned down, it would look like sour grapes rather than a clear decision on principle. I could also foresee considerable speculation about my future action and wished to act as early as I could.

My friends at Westminster argued against early resignation. They said that its impact on the Party Conference would be harmful to the causes we all had at heart. They thought that the reaction of the ordinary Party members against me, and, by association, against them, would prejudice any possibility of a compromise vote on British entry into the Common Market. Roy Jenkins's own standing with delegates at the Conference would be affected. For all this I would get the blame. While I was not unduly worried about being unpopular, since I did not expect to be the darling of the Labour movement after my resignation, the other points did seem to have some force. If the Conference turned out to be a victory for the extreme left this might help my own election campaign. But on the critical issue of Britain's position in Europe the adoption of a compromise formula, however weak or dishonest, would clearly be better than a straight rejection of the Common Market and a clear commitment to withdrawal by a future Labour Government.

Although I was doubtful how far my resignation would influence any of these events, I had no wish to cause unnecessary embarrassment to my friends.

I therefore agreed to postpone a decision on the timing of my resignation, to consult my Lincoln Committee further and to come to a final decision after the summer holidays. Some of the Jenkinsites were obviously hoping that this period of reflection might change my mind about the whole venture. But in this kind of situation one must trust one's own judgment. I had made up my mind and I stuck to my decision to fight.

I decided to announce my resignation on October 6th, 1972, at the end of the Party Conference, to hold a meeting in Lincoln shortly afterwards at which I could explain the reasons for my actions to my constituents and to apply for the stewardship of the Manor of Northstead on October 16th. This was one of the two 'offices of profit under the Crown' (in fact unpaid) for which an M.P. traditionally applied as a means of resigning.

The date of the by-election itself was not something within my own control. Parliamentary convention, agreed between the main parties since 1911, declares that the Chief Whip of the party which last held the seat applies for the writ for a by-election. He can delay the date as long as he likes. If a Back Bench M.P. were to move the writ and if the motion for it should be defeated (a likely result because of the agreement between the parties), the writ cannot be moved again in the same session. There is no good reason why this rule should not be changed and a time limit set within which a by-election must be held. In fact the Labour Party moved the writ early in February 1973 and the by-election was held on March 1st, 1973.

I announced my resignation at a press conference in the House of Commons. A few hours later I had gained an unexpected ally in securing publicity for my campaign. In his winding-up speech at the Party Conference the Chairman, Anthony Wedgwood Benn, went out of his way to denounce me. My electoral description, as decided at Lincoln, was 'Democratic Labour'. Benn said I was neither Democratic nor Labour, that I was a candidate invented by the media and that the

Labour movement would take on and defeat this new threat to democracy in the same way in which they had defeated kings and landowners in the past. The printers should see to it that the truth was published about Labour and even the liftmen in Thomson House should play their part (in a way still to be defined). Later he explained that he never meant to suggest that printers should seek to influence what was printed. His extraordinary outburst was shown time after time on the television screen.

I found the support from people in Lincoln most encouraging from the very start. Journalists had been sceptical about my chances, largely because all the precedents were against me. The *Sunday Times*, for example, talked about my suicidal action. But an opinion poll taken in Lincoln for the television programme *Weekend World* on the day after my resignation gave me a huge lead. Those who said they would vote for me were 49 per cent, for the Conservatives 16 per cent and for Labour 14 per cent. Eliminating 'Don't knows' and others, that gave me about 63 per cent, the Conservatives 20 per cent and Labour 17 per cent. It seemed too good to be true. It was probably this poll which persuaded the Labour Party to postpone the election date as long as possible so that the emotions aroused by my resignation would die down.

When the date was finally announced in February 1973 I certainly felt that I had lost some of those who supported me in October. But this was bound to happen once the two Party machines were fully organized in support of their official candidates. I knew some doubters on both sides would be drawn back by the call of Party loyalty. I also feared that others would in the end regard the issues of the day, such as unemployment, the first effects of membership of the European Community, the rise in prices or the behaviour of the unions, as more important than the rather unusual cause I was championing. There was a risk that once the traditional Tory-versus-Labour battle was engaged, the electorate would see the issues in terms of Government and Opposition, with an Independent helpless to influence events.

On the other hand, the delay had given me time to build up an organization based on the experience of some of the old hands from Grafton House who had left with me. A healthy inflow of funds from sympathizers had made it possible to employ a full-time Agent, Tony Elkington, who showed great flair and imagination, and a charming and efficient secretary, Ann Venn. Tony Elkington had also found a disused billiard hall, well situated in the centre of Lincoln, which he transformed into a cheap but reasonably suitable campaign headquarters. He and the other members of the Democratic Labour Association, which we founded, decided to call it Taverne House. I found this embarrassing but could see that it was a cheap way of keeping the candidate's name before the public. An effective organization was of enormous value, and our organization soon became far more effective, as far as I could judge, than that of either of the two main parties, which had to rely heavily on helpers from outside Lincoln. Supporters came flooding in to us, of all ages (though mainly young), of all parties and none, and nearly all full of enthusiasm. Two comments made by outsiders are worth recording. One journalist said the atmosphere reminded him of the campaign by Senator Eugene McCarthy for the Presidency in 1968. *The Economist* remarked on the way in which Conservative matrons worked side by side with shop stewards, whom they would have regarded as dangerous subversives only a few months before.

Even if the delay between my resignation and polling day did slightly decrease my eventual majority, as it may have done, it enabled us to lay foundations for the future which were even more important than extra votes. My own assessment was that the Labour Party miscalculated in putting off the election and did themselves long-term harm.

In the event neither of the main parties fought a very brilliant campaign. The Conservatives were very quiet. Their candidate, Jonathan Guinness, sparkled at press conferences. One reporter told me that he did not know which he found the more entertaining: Guinness's witty cracks or watching his experienced Agent wince. Some of his sallies, however, made him look inexperienced and eccentric and he made little impact on the doorstep.

The Labour Party recovered a certain amount of support, mainly through the huge effort made and the flood of helpers that poured in. I was told that over a hundred Members of Parliament came down to Lincoln, more than had been known in almost any by-election. Other workers came in from every part of the country. We saw Labour canvassers everywhere and they were never people we knew.

The electoral strategy of the Labour candidate, John Dilks, and his advisers, seemed to me inept. They could not decide whether to go for personal attacks or to ignore me. In the end they compromised by trying both—personal attacks from November to the middle of January, talking about issues solely and acting as if I did not exist until near the end of February, and back to personal attacks again in the final week.

My own campaign had two themes: a particular one centred on the position of a Member of Parliament, and a wider one linked with the disillusionment in politics caused by the two main parties. At the beginning the first theme was the main one: I emphasized that a Member of Parliament should stand by his electoral commitments, that he should refuse to accept dictation from a caucus and that he was a representative rather than a delegate. The second theme became more prominent as the campaign developed, partly in reaction to what Guinness and Dilks were saying. I stressed the need to reject the double talk of the main parties, to avoid the extremism both of the Monday Club, of which Guinness was Chairman, and of the far-left wing at Grafton House; I concentrated on the need to combine a prices and incomes policy, which the Labour Party now denounced, with social justice which the Government was unable to provide. I also argued in favour of industrial democracy and against strikes. The Common Market was a relatively minor issue, but clearly my support for Britain's entry did not lose me many votes—contrary to the deepest convictions of Grafton House. I tried to use the issues raised by my opponents to illustrate the need for what I called a social democratic approach.

What worried me most in the campaign was that during this period two groups of workers were on strike: gas workers and hospital ancillary workers. Both groups were lower-paid workers. Both strikes were directed against the Government's incomes policy. Seen against the background of increasing industrial unrest and the inconvenience caused by the miners as well as the railway strike the year before, there was little doubt about the unpopularity of these strikes. I was afraid that those who opposed the strikers might therefore vote Conservative and those who sympathized with low-paid workers might vote Labour. I could be squeezed out the more the feelings were aroused and became polarized.

Our public meetings were very well attended from the start, and both major themes were well received. My first meeting, on October 15th, to explain my resignation, was the biggest meeting I can recall at Lincoln—four hundred and fifty people in the hall and some two hundred and fifty turned away. The opening meeting of the campaign, when I was most excellently supported by the Bishop of Southwark and Bernard Levin, drew about four hundred and fifty people. Our final meeting, when my old friend The Rev. Stanley Booth-Clibborn spoke, was attended by close on four hundred people and was perhaps the most successful meeting of all. The suggestion that we were possibly starting something new, first explicitly raised by Bernard Levin, drew increasing support and applause as the campaign went on.

One event that seemed to make a definite impact on the electorate was a long programme arranged by Anglia Television, which was shown on the final Monday of the campaign. I had been doubtful about agreeing to appear together with all the candidates. This was for tactical reasons: I was, after all, well known to the electorate, whereas Guinness and Dilks were not. I did not think that my greater experience of television would be a big advantage, since a television debate is a great leveller. Even if I should prove to have the edge in the debates, I suspected that Guinness and Dilks would perform better than people expected and therefore seem to show up well. Lastly I feared that it would all turn out as showbiz, an exhibition rather than serious politics, because of the presence of fringe candidates like Reg Simmerson, 'Democratic Conservative against the Common Market', Malcolm Waller, who stood for majority rule by referendum, and Mr Jean Justice, whose platform was that Hanratty was wrongly hanged. However, I also felt that it would be a dog-in-the-manger attitude to refuse to appear on a joint platform and that it would seem inconsistent for a 'Democratic' candidate, who argued that principle should come before tactics, to put tactical consideration first. I therefore agreed to take part. All the candidates except Mr Waller, who could not come, faced a studio audience and answered questions.

After the programme, our canvassers found that many electors who had previously been undecided had come down in my favour. While Guinness had looked somewhat stiff and expressionless, Dilks was unpleasant, like an overblown ham-actor playing the role of the ordinary man who understands the people. I felt relaxed, having prepared for the programme with two hours' sleep.

We won even more handsomely than I had expected. At the lowest point of the campaign, before the last big effort which I had delayed deliberately until a week before polling, I feared that we might win by only four to five thousand votes. By the end I was sure we were in by about eight thousand votes. The actually majority of thirteen thousand took all except my Agent by surprise. What I had not expected, until I saw the overwhelming effort put into their campaign, was that the Labour Party would push the Conservatives into third place. It seems I received roughly 60 per cent of the former Labour votes and about the same proportion of former Tories'. The figures, 58 per cent, 23 per cent and 18 per cent, were not very different from those of the opinion poll taken in October.

I can still only guess at the main reasons for my victory. My work in the constituency for ten and a half years as Member of Parliament may have helped, but I suspect only marginally. The most common reaction found by canvassers on the doorstep was that people liked a man who stuck to his guns. This was certainly what I found in my own handshaking tours of the city. The unpopularity of 'that lot in Grafton House' helped me considerably. The extremism of their views was as unpopular in the factories as on the doorstep. Disillusionment with both main parties also emerged strongly—'You can't believe a word they say.'

I believe that it would be a mistake to attribute the result of the Lincoln by-election entirely to the unusual circumstances which had brought it about and which at first sight might be thought to be the principal reason for my victory. A stand for principle made an impact because it contrasted so strongly with the prevailing attitudes that the Party must always come first. A reasonable approach to politics, which I tried to convey, one of moderation combined with a desire for social justice, contrasted with the dogma and the class-conscious militancy of the Labour left wing which the leading figures at Grafton House personified. Time after time we heard the Granada *World in Action* programme mentioned although it was shown nearly one and a half years before.* It made a profound impact on the consciousness of Lincoln because the reaction of the dedicated left-wingers, faced, as they saw it, with a 'right-wing deviationist' within the Party, and one who was a middle-class intellectual to boot, was revealed by television in all its unattractive bitterness.

The result of the by-election did, I think, show how little public support the left wing of the Labour Party commands. Many of the 8,800 people who voted Labour did so because they had always done so. Only a small proportion, I would guess, voted Labour because they agreed with the political philosophy of Grafton House. Certainly no one who shared the views of Grafton House would have supported me. If the left wing were capable of realism the Lincoln story would give them much to think about. Being what they are, they blamed it on the media.

* See Chapter 4, p. 61.

PART II: AFTER

7
DIAGNOSIS

The Lincoln story is one particular illustration of the conflicts between social democrats and the left wing of the Labour Party. It ended in Lincoln in March 1973 with a resounding defeat for the latter. I believe one is entitled to infer from its outcome that if the Tribune Group dominates the Labour Party and dictates its policies, the future of the Labour Party is bleak.

My political friends in the Labour Party would probably accept this inference. They would also accept that the influence of the Tribune Group inside the Party today is too great for Labour's electoral health. They do not, however, regard the present balance of power as more than a temporary misfortune. In time the Party will, they feel, return to sanity. If it wins the next General Election, the social democrats will come into their rightful heritage once more, partly because much administrative talent is to be found within their ranks which will enable them to work their way back into the key positions of power, and partly because, in practice, any future Labour Government would be forced by circumstances to pursue a policy of moderate rather than extreme socialism. If Labour loses the next election, they would expect, and certainly hope for, a reaction against the left-wing mood which now prevails. The ordinary Party worker would realize that at the instigation of the Tribune Group, the Party had gone a-whoring after false gods.

I regard neither of these two scenarios as likely to happen. If Labour wins the election, a number of left-wingers would inevitably occupy key positions in the Government as the right wing of the Party has no monopoly of administrative talent. These left-wingers will not lightly abandon the programme which the Labour Party now advocates. It is, no doubt, correct to make the prognosis that some of the main policies now proposed would prove impossible to implement (for instance, any government would, I suspect, be bound to impose statutory controls on income); but the reaction of the rank and file would not consist of a placid acceptance of realism and responsibility. Instead, there would be felt a sense of betrayal more violent than that felt during the Labour Government of 1964–70, and this might build up to a catastrophe for the Party. If, on the other hand, Labour loses the election, I regard a further swing to the Left, or an uneasy compromise, as more likely than a return to social democracy. I shall examine these possibilities more fully in Chapter 11.

I am not so much concerned in this book with the immediate electoral prospects of the Labour Party as with the longer-term future of the Left. Since I believe there is something basically wrong with the Labour Party, rather than that it is going through a bad patch, I feel we may be approaching one of those periods in British politics when existing party alignments break up and re-form. Sometimes in the past one major issue has so deeply divided a party as to cause it to split; the Corn Laws led to the Peelite revolt from the Tories, and Irish Home Rule led to the secession of Chamberlain from the Liberals. At other times a major social change has induced a corresponding political change: the decline of the Liberal Party earlier this century, and its replacement by the Labour Party, was linked with the rise in the power and influence of the trade unions, who allied themselves with Labour rather than with the Liberals. The by-elections of 1973 have already suggested that the party political scene is far more fluid than at any time since the war.

It is not impossible that Britain's role in Europe will prove to be an issue with the same cataclysmic effect on the Labour Party as the Corn Laws had on the Tories in the last century. It would be a mistake to underestimate the impact which the argument about Europe has already had on the balance of power within the Party, or the disadvantage at which a radical party is placed if it does not frame its policies within the European context. I shall argue in the next chapter that Britain's full participation in the European Community is essential if we are to control our own economic destiny. If Labour remains chauvinistic and insular in its attitude, it will become a party irrelevant to the major problems of our time and will wither as a force for radicalism.

There is another even more fundamental reason why I am doubtful about the future of Labour as the main party of the Left. Its links with the unions, which were originally the cause of its emergence as a major political force, may also prove to be the cause of its decline. Earlier this century the class struggle was at its height. The unions were fighting for the rights of the working man, and their fight was also the fight for liberty, equality and social justice. While the unions today still play an important role, they do not always promote social justice by their activities. In some areas of industry they are still struggling to raise wages which are intolerably low and to protect the dignity of employees. Exploitation of female labour is an obvious example of such an area. In general, however, free collective bargaining by the unions has created, and perpetuates, differentials in wages between different groups of workers which many will regard as unjust. The unions, moreover, will not accept measures to control the level of wage increases, measures which are in my view an indispensable part of any effective policy against inflation. In the longer run, I foresee a change too in the attitude of our society to the rights of producers and consumers. So far we have been dominated by the needs of the producers. Both the major political parties are financed by the producers' organizations: the Tories, by organized business, and the Labour party, by organized labour. But the balance of power may shift against producers, as industrial societies are forced to re-examine their obsession with the maximum growth of their Gross National Product. There could be a major conflict of interests between a radical party of the future that represents the consumer or the unorganized citizen and the forces of organized labour.

Under the Labour Party's constitution, power rests with the unions. When the Party is in government, power passes in practice to the Cabinet, which can propose (even if it does not always implement) measures to which the unions are opposed. In Opposition, however, the freedom of the Shadow Cabinet, or indeed of the Parliamentary Party, to act independently of the unions is severely circumscribed, in practice as well as in theory. The Party may therefore find itself tied inextricably to an interest group which, in the changed circumstances of modern society, will increasingly prevent the Party from developing a radical philosophy suitable to our times. This theme is more fully developed in Chapter 10.

In the chapters which follow I have made no attempt to list the detailed programme which a radical party should pursue; nor have I tried to set out a comprehensive philosophy for social democracy in the 'seventies.

People should not expect too much from politicians. We are not, most of us, originators of ideas. Our task, if we are competent at our job, is to be well informed, to pick and choose sensibly from the ideas of others and to make use of their expertise. We should judge which proposals have a chance of being effective. Our job is then to persuade, to fight for some courses of action and against others, sometimes to represent popular opinion and sometimes, perhaps, to oppose it. Ideally a Member of Parliament should stand up firmly and boldly for the values he believes in, even when he is under pressure. But a politician certainly does not have to be a don, an efficiency expert, a lawyer, an accountant or an economist, or an expert in industrial relations, in order to discuss or advocate the ideas which the experts advance. What is more, he is unlikely to be a philosopher. Political philosophers, like other philosophers, are rare in Parliament. One of the few Members of Parliament who have made any major contribution to political thought is Tony Crosland with his book *The Future of Socialism*, written in 1956. I could certainly not attempt to rival that formidable work.

In the following chapters I will consider only those issues which I judge likely to have a profound influence on the politics of the Left. I will examine first the reasons why responsible attitudes to Britain's role in Europe are vital to the future of the Labour Party. Next I will try to analyse the central features of the Party's constitution, since part of the present unhappy state of the Party may be traced to its constitution. I shall then discuss in greater detail how far the social effects of the activities of the unions have changed since the Labour Party was founded and whether they are compatible with the aims of a radical party today.

Finally, I will draw the different strands together and will seek to assess how far, despite its handicaps, the Labour Party is nevertheless the best means we have for achieving radical change or whether there are good prospects for an alternative.

8

EUROPE

The moment Labour had lost the 1970 election, several of the social democrats in the Parliamentary Labour Party foresaw that the issue of British entry into the European Community could prove a very dangerous one both for the Party and for their own position within it. At the end of June 1970 some of the leading pro-Marketeers met at my flat in Kensington. They included Roy Jenkins, George Thomson, Bill Rodgers, David Owen, David Marquand and others. We discussed what attitude the Labour Party was likely to adopt towards British entry and whether or not Roy Jenkins should stand for the Deputy Leadership of the Party. The two questions were to some extent linked because the case against Roy Jenkins standing was that his election might limit his freedom to promote his views about Europe. If the Party leaders came out against entry, it was argued that he should keep himself free to take a different line. Most of us felt that he should stand, since as Deputy Leader he would be in a much more powerful position to seek to prevent an adverse decision, or, at the worst, to prevent opposition to entry becoming a complete rejection of Europe.

No one could be certain what Harold Wilson's attitude would be. Lest I should attribute to my colleagues views which they did not hold or voice, I shall record only my own impressions at the time. I was, and am, convinced that when he was Prime Minister, Harold Wilson became genuinely converted to the cause of the European Community. One only has to reread his speeches in the 1967 debate on the Common Market in Parliament to see the strength of his commitment. When Wilson said, as he did at the time, 'We shall not take "No" for an answer,' he did not, one feels, mean us to infer that the answer 'Yes' might prove to be equally unacceptable. Nor can this remark simply be brushed aside, as he has sought to do since, by explaining that he referred only to the opening of negotiations. The implication was clearly one of an absolute determination that Britain should join the E.E.C. if at all possible.

The Labour Party manifesto for the 1970 General Election was much more definite than the Party now cares to admit. It said that 'we meant business' in the negotiations which were about to start. This could have only one interpretation: no one could mean business if he intended to reopen matters which had already been finalized by the six existing members after long and difficult discussions, and which they clearly had no intention of reopening. The Common Agricultural Policy, for example, could not be reformulated as part of the negotiations for entry, although it would certainly need to be modified once we were members ourselves. The same was true of the commitment to a Value Added Tax. The agricultural regulations and the system for financing the European Budget had also finally been agreed by the end of 1969. The main items open to negotiation in 1970 were the transitional arrangements for finance; providing for continued dairy exports from New Zealand; and guaranteeing sufficient exports of Commonwealth sugar. If Harold Wilson in 1970 had held the views which he professes to hold today about the disadvantages of the Common Market, he would never have agreed to start negotiating at all.

Despite, as I saw it, his genuine conversion to the cause of Europe, I thought nevertheless that it was likely that Harold Wilson after 1970 would find reasons for voting against British entry, whatever terms were obtained. The two leading unions, the Engineers and the Transport Workers, were almost certain to oppose entry under any conditions. Their leaders Hugh Scanlon and Jack Jones were both opposed to British entry. The left wing of the Parliamentary Party, with a few exceptions, were likewise against it. (The exceptions like Eric Heffer soon joined up with the other anti-Marketeers in the Tribune Group.) Ordinary Party members throughout the country might have accepted the prospect of British entry under a Labour Government, as they seemed ready to do in 1967; the odds were, however, that in the absence of strong leadership from Wilson, the majority would not accept it under a Conservative Government. According to the opinion polls, popular feeling was against British entry. If Harold Wilson had stuck to his previous policy, he would have faced a split Party as well as a hostile electorate. I could imagine his fears that he might not only lose the leadership of the Party but see it committed totally against the principle of entry, irrespective of the terms. If, on the other hand, he could lead the Party into qualified opposition, he might preserve its unity and also protect the pro-Marketeers from being driven into the wilderness. Later, when Labour came back to power with Britain safely inside the Community, the new Labour Government would probably accept entry as a *fait accompli*. It was a line of policy that required some tactical acrobatics – but at these he excelled. I believe that this was originally the strategy he meant to follow, and to some extent would like to follow still.

The case against this course of action by Wilson was that it was likely both to destroy his credibility and to prove unsuccessful. In the first place, people do not admire a man who changes his mind for tactical advantage, even when he does so to come over to their side. Wilson has suffered from the fact that people do not believe what he says. The weakness has become more serious in the course of time. Appearing to change his stand on such a major issue as the Common Market, and voting against what people knew he used to be for, has perhaps done more to destroy his credibility than anything else.

Secondly, it was unlikely that any appeasement of the extreme anti-Europeans would assuage their appetite for outright opposition. They would simply gobble up concessions and ask for more. It was also a course of action that would switch the balance of power in the Party from the social democrats, who largely favoured entry, to the Tribune Group, who totally opposed it. Wilson must have realized that if the Labour Party were seen to be dominated by Michael Foot and his friends, it would look less like a viable alternative government. Handing power over to them, by supporting them over Europe, would in the end prove just as damaging to the Party as a major split.

The alternative strategy, which Harold Wilson ought to have followed, was to fight. It would have required a determination to 'fight, fight and fight again', like Hugh Gaitskell; confidence that the Parliamentary Labour Party would make an independent stand; and faith that he could win Conference round in the end. This is hardly Wilson's style. He had, after all, opposed Gaitskell for the leadership after the 1960 Scarborough Conference precisely because he thought a leader's duty was to avert the wrath of the rank and file, and not to face it head on. Wilson, it seemed to me, would be temperamentally incapable of adopting the only strategy that might both save himself losing credibility and avoid permanent damage to the Party.

During the course of time Wilson's attitude to British membership of the E.E.C. has become increasingly hostile. In October 1971 he imposed a Three-Line Whip ordering all Labour M.P.s to vote against the Government on the day when Parliament made the decision whether Britain should join. He was hoping to win the vote with the help of Conservative rebels, and defeating the Government was more important to him than the future of Britain in Europe. He must have known that if Parliament had voted against Europe on the day, it would have closed the door on British membership of the E.E.C. once and for all. During the passage through Parliament of the European Community Bill, which was required to make our entry effective for the purposes of British law and the British constitution, Wilson appointed Michael Foot and Peter Shore as Labour's official spokesmen, thus ensuring that the arguments advanced by the Opposition would be based on opposition in principle. Later he himself made speeches about the surrender of our parliamentary sovereignty to Brussels, which suggested that he was rejecting the principles on which the Community is based. He also supported a boycott of the Community institutions, such as the European Parliament at Strasbourg, pending

Labour's return to power and the renegotiation which Labour promised. As expected, the root-and-branch opponents of entry are still not satisfied with Labour's position; they seek an unqualified undertaking that Britain should withdraw.

It is more than probable that Wilson still hopes to avoid initiating Britain's withdrawal from the European Community if he wins the next General Election. The Labour Party is at present committed to a renegotiation of the terms of entry; but the difference between renegotiating terms of entry (which under the Treaty of Rome cannot be done) and negotiating to modify Community arrangements (which happens all the time between Community members) is a fine one for the public to grasp. Wilson would, in my view, aim simply to negotiate for modification, without perhaps attending too sedulously to the terms for renegotiation imposed on him by Conference resolutions.* According to the official policy of the Party, a Labour Government would also be committed to consult the British people by a referendum or by a General Election about the results of the renegotiations. If Wilson wins the next election, I can foresee that the negotiating process would be drawn out for nearly a full parliamentary term. Some concessions would no doubt be granted by the Community. A Labour Government might then justifiably claim a measure of success. And in due course, since a General Election would be near, it might reasonably propose that public opinion should be tested by a General Election rather than by a referendum, a system which is, in any event, alien to British parliamentary traditions. The public would then be given a choice between a Labour Party which advocated that Britain should not withdraw from the Community and a Conservative Party which advocated that Britain should remain within. Pledges, he would doubtless claim, would have been honoured.

This may be what Harold Wilson would like to do, but it is questionable whether the outright opponents of British member-

* Compare the pre-1964 pledge which Wilson gave to renegotiate the Nassau Agreement under which the United States undertook the supply of Britain's Polaris missiles. The renegotiation never took place.

ship will allow him. They have gained too powerful a hold on the Party machine and have made too many converts in the rank and file of Party activists. A Labour Cabinet, which would almost certainly include Michael Foot, Peter Shore and Anthony Wedgwood Benn, could hardly be expected to abandon overnight all its deep reservations about the Community or the solemn undertakings which have been given to the Labour movement. In any event, there is another reason why it is unlikely that the anti-European tide will flow less strongly before the next election: the attitude of Enoch Powell.

As I have already mentioned, there are many issues on which Enoch Powell and the left wing agree. The mutual admiration of Foot and Powell is great. They share a passionate devotion to Parliament, which they seek to protect from the depredations of Parliamentary reformers and pro-Europeans alike. They are self-appointed guardians of Parliament's traditions, who reject any idea that Parliament should make more use of Select Committees in order to enable M.P.s to become better informed, and believe instead in government by oratory on the floor of the House. Above all, they attribute to Parliament a supreme sovereignty which it may have in law but cannot exercise in practice, and see the transfer of power to Brussels, or even to the European Parliament in Strasbourg, as an act close to treason. Powell, the arch-Conservative, is now even prepared to consider the idea of inviting his supporters to vote Labour.

The temptations to many leading figures in the Labour Party must be almost irresistible. They knew that Powell's following in the country is considerable. He is easily the most popular leading figure among the Conservatives, with a keen following among Labour voters as well. Many people in the Labour Party feel that he played a major part in winning the last election for the Conservatives, especially by his appeal in constituencies in the Midlands. They may by now, after Lincoln and a string of Liberal by-election victories, realize that support for Europe is no insuperable obstacle to winning elections, nor opposition to Europe a key to electoral success. Nevertheless a call by Powell to vote Labour, whatever the reasons, could at the least neutralize a large section of the Conservative vote in the Midlands, and might even affect the result elsewhere.

To achieve this glittering prize, Labour leaders would not need to compromise with Powell on immigration, or public ownership. All they have to do is to make clear in Labour's election manifesto that unless certain conditions are obtained, Britain will withdraw from the Community. This is in any event official Labour policy. The tougher the conditions, the more likely the Powellite secession from the Tories.

Britain's role in Europe may therefore still become an issue that creates new alignments in British politics. If Labour carried out in power the programme to which it is literally committed in opposition, withdrawal from the Community might still happen. Political forces from within and the temptations of winning Powellite support outside may make it harder to avoid implementing the literal commitment than many commentators now suppose. If so, the loyalty of pro-Europeans in the Labour Party may be strained beyond the breaking-point. On the other hand there are other factors at work which militate ever more strongly against any possible withdrawal. With every day that passes, the trade unions are becoming more deeply involved in Community institutions. Within a few years, too, British industry will be so closely interlocked with Europe that a withdrawal from Europe ceases to be a feasible policy for rational men.

Even if the Labour Party avoids a break with the Community, its present policies towards Europe disqualify the Party from making a relevant contribution to some of the biggest problems of our time. No radical party can ignore the European context within which so much of Britain's policy should be framed.

I have never argued the case in favour of Britain's entry into the Common Market primarily on economic grounds. Indeed, the combination of higher food prices and the additional burden on the balance of payments caused by our payments to the Agricultural Fund seemed to me strong arguments against entry which offset many of the advantages to industry. I am not surprised that academic economists were almost evenly divided for and against. While political and economic arguments cannot be neatly divorced, those arguments which I have found convincing are either political, or ones where politics and economics are intertwined. They can be summed up in the general proposition that many of our important problems are too big to be solved on a national scale and that only on the Community level is a workable solution possible.

Let me take the example of our policy on energy. I am not qualified to judge whether or not the supplies of energy will prove to be enough for the needs of the world in ten or twenty years' time. I suspect that with good sense and management we can avoid a crisis, although, in the past, demand seems to have been consistently underestimated. However, certain facts have emerged. First, oil is now being consumed at a faster rate than new reserves are being discovered. This is likely to lead to a more restrictive attitude to the production of oil on the part of states like Saudi-Arabia which own the largest reserves. On present patterns of development it seems more than likely that by the early or middle 1980s the economics of the developed world will no longer be able to rely on traditional sources of fuel being available in sufficient quantity to meet all their needs. Nuclear energy has so far been regarded as the main alternative, but its supply on a large scale presents many unsolved problems, including the disposal of radioactive wastes. Time required to solve these problems, if they can be solved at all, will delay the building of the nuclear power-stations, and they themselves take a long time to build. As a result we are likely to need nuclear energy before it becomes available. We cannot count on alternative sources of energy such as solar energy being developed in time. Nor can the renewed exploitation of coal provide the answer.

Whatever the exact picture in the 1980s, one can surely predict that there will be severe competition between the advanced industrial nations for the supplies of oil that are available. It has already started. The United States and Japan are determined to secure the maximum share for themselves. European countries like Britain, despite the prospect of oil from the North Sea, will still be dependent on the Middle Eastern supplies; but if European countries act separately they will be placed behind the largest customers at the end of the queue. Only if the European Community acts as one unit will it be able to bargain with the United States and Japan. It would be disastrous for each European nation to make its own deal, since that could be done only at the expense of other Community members. If national interests are not forgone in the interests of the Community, 'the lights may well go out all over Europe'.* National interests themselves require that no one member of the Community should have the power of veto in the Council of Ministers over decisions about the sharing of oil supplies and that Community internationalism should flourish instead.

Another example of a field that requires an international approach is that of the international companies. I can think of no area where official Labour Party thinking is more self-contradictory. First, power and influence is ascribed to these companies in such measure as to make them appear to be the controllers of modern society who conspire to defeat the aspirations of mankind towards social justice. Their influence is seen in Manichean terms. Secondly, the remedy for this abuse of power is sought in national measures of control by a future Labour Government in Britain. The picture of their power seems as exaggerated as the remedy suggested would be inappropriate and ineffective.

The behaviour and influence of international companies (perhaps more commonly known as multi-nationals) is a subject on its own. A recent study of I.T.T. by Anthony Sampson† does not describe a company that has been a paragon of social virtue or one that has shown exceptional sensitivity to the interests of its host nations; but it would be a mistake to regard all the multinationals as malefactors. In most countries where they have settled they have helped economic development; they have certainly made a valuable contribution to exports from Britain,

* See the report of the Committee on Energy of the European Parliament, dated May 6th, 1972.

† *The Sovereign State: The Secret History of I.T.T.* (Hodder & Stoughton, London, 1973).

and they have helped to improve managerial techniques. I believe that in general they have shown themselves considerate of the wishes and susceptibilities of host governments. On the other hand, there can be no doubt that their own interests and those of the host government do not necessarily coincide. The tax liability of multi-nationals has often been organized so that in different countries it contrasts favourably with that of their mono-national competitors. Host governments are thus deprived of much-needed revenue. Their bargaining power with national governments is considerable. They can play off the incentives to investment offered in one country against those offered in another. They can ignore the regional policies of governments by threatening to go abroad if they are not allowed to settle where they wish. They subject themselves to democratic control as often by voluntary agreement as because of the power of sovereign states. There is no doubt that their increasing power prevents proper political control over the economic affairs of a country *if* political power can be exercised only at national level.

How can national policy in a country like Britain effectively control the multi-nationals? No doubt a company like Ford has no desire to lose its large investments in Dagenham or Merseyside; but it has other fish to fry. If its British subsidiaries become unprofitable, or much less profitable, it will concentrate its efforts elsewhere. In some cases production plans have already been transferred to other countries because of labour troubles in Britain. Sometimes a multi-national may be less sensitive to industrial pressures from unions than are its national rivals.* At other times multi-nationals will be less sensitive to government measures seeking to enforce resistance to pay claims. Certainly, national control of the money supply is not likely to affect local subsidiaries of multi-national companies to the same extent as it affects national firms.

Almost by definition, control of international companies demands international control, and the only international body

* During a recent strike at Dagenham the unions appealed to the German motorcar workers in Ford, Germany, to support them. These sent back a message which said, in effect, 'We are all behind you. Please keep on striking.'

with sufficient political cohesion to develop such control is the European Community. It would be an illusion to pretend that the Community already has the power. It can prevent certain kinds of restrictive practices; it may soon develop an effective policy against monopolies and a more uniform approach to regional incentives; but there is no early prospect of a common company law or a single system of corporate taxation; and, above all, the political institutions which can exercise political control over economic forces have not yet developed. It does not, unfortunately, follow from the fact that if national control has been eroded, international control will take its place. For a variety of irrational, mainly nationalistic, reasons, international anarchy—by which I mean the absence of political control—may prevail instead. What is clear is that we face a choice between a passive acceptance of such anarchy, or promoting the political unity of the European Community.

My third example of an area requiring concerted international action is that concerning monetary matters. The monetary crises which the Western world has recently experienced have had a major impact on national economic policies, and these crises cannot be controlled by a national government acting alone. The values of currencies change more widely, and more rapidly, than the underlying economic strength or weakness of the countries involved. Germany has been forced to revalue the Mark time after time—contrary to her own wishes and her longer-term economic interests—as a result of the flow of millions of Eurodollars across the exchanges. Britain has repeatedly found her economic problems aggravated by international monetary flows. We have suffered from the whims of speculators as well as from the follies of ministers. Recently, the best-laid plans of finance ministers and central bankers have gone awry at ever-decreasing intervals. Each 'final solution' has proved more temporary than the last. Not for forty years has the international monetary system been so unstable.

Once again, it would be an illusion to suggest that the existence of the Community alone is sufficient to solve the problem. In some ways the present half-way stage, where the member states of the Community seek a common solution but cannot agree, is the worst of all. It produces weak compromises where we need radical change. The Bretton Woods Agreement, which ensured the broad monetary stability of the post-war period, was made possible because the negotiating partners that mattered were few. At the moment there are too many, and there seems little doubt that the monetary union of Europe would be a valuable contribution towards monetary stability. It would reduce the main bargaining parties to three: Europe, the United States and Japan. Nor would this be an undesirable 'carve-up' of the world. Monetary instability caused by the flow of speculative funds is a disease of the advanced industrial nations of the West and of Japan. It must be solved by them, although it should certainly be solved in such a way that the reserves of the developing world are strengthened rather than depleted.

I recognize that the European Monetary Union neither guarantees solutions to international monetary problems nor can exist without its dangers for Britain. As it would deprive members of the Union of the freedom to alter the exchange rates of their currencies, it would require a much closer assimilation of the rates of economic growth and the rates of domestic inflation of all member states than one has any right to expect by 1980. I regard the target date of 1980 for achieving monetary union as unrealistic and designed more as a spur to action than an expectation of what can be achieved. However, the process of moving towards monetary union improves the chances of a genuinely common approach to the reform of the international system.

There are many other issues which require international, not national, solutions. A common approach to our environment is an obvious case. I am not just referring to the need for measures for the control of pollution in the atmosphere or in the rivers. At present, the effects of industrial pollution in one country can wreck the policies for protecting the environment which are promoted by another. It is also true that nation states cannot take certain kinds of desirable measures individually for fear of placing themselves at a disadvantage with their competitors.

Britain, for example, might wish to legislate for safer and longer-lasting motor-cars. There is no reason why cars should be deliberately designed for obsolescence, to last for only seven to ten years. Scrapped cars pollute the countryside, and built-in obsolescence is a scandalous waste of resources. However, if British regulations provided in effect that no cars could be driven on British roads which had not been built to last thirty years, motor manufacturers in Britain might be driven out of business. Such measures would be politically feasible or effective only if taken by all nations, or at least by a group of nations which can stand on its own. If the European Community passed regulations of this kind, their impact on the exports of Japan or even the United States might be enough to abolish deliberate waste in making motor-cars throughout the world.

Lastly, effective action to help the Third World needs joint action by the developed countries. The General Scheme for Preferences adopted by the European Community shows what might be achieved. In itself, the scheme does not achieve its object of boosting the exports of developing countries to Europe by giving these exports preferential treatment. Quotas are fixed on a formula which leaves little room for expansion. The list of goods to which preferential treatment is given is too restrictive. But the scheme could be amended and developed to be of great benefit to the Third World's trade. Britain's own efforts, even if they were to compare favourably with the record of other countries, are infinitely less significant than the combined policies of the whole European Community.

It can be argued by those who fear the possibility of a European Federation that in all these fields—sources of energy, multi-national companies, monetary policy, the environment, and policies towards the developing world—co-ordination between national governments can and must provide the answer. If it cannot, then we must frankly face the implications: the emergence of a European super-state with federal power in which Britain and the other European countries become mere provinces. Indeed, we must face the fundamental question, which was passed over somewhat lightly during the 'great debate' about Britain's entry, 'What kind of community have we joined and how do we wish to see it develop?'

It is hard to see how co-ordination between states can ever effectively solve the problems I have outlined. National governments are responsible to national parliaments, which are reluctant to see short-term national interests overruled. They will not give Ministers a completely free hand in negotiations. From time to time they will insist that British representatives take a British rather than a Community view, even when Community interests—for the reasons already given—may well be more in line with the long-term interests of all the member states. Sometimes any common solution will be better than none. While national power of veto still exists, it will often be used to prevent there being any solution. I regard internationalist answers as inevitable.

This does not, however, mean the early establishment of a United States of Europe to rival the United States of America. Those who fear or advocate a federation of the classical type for Europe need to reflect on history. None of the historic ingredients which have created other federations are present in Europe. There has been no war of independence against a colonial power; there is no longer an overwhelming fear of powerful neighbours. There is no common sense of nationhood, no common language and no common sense of history (except of conflict between European states). The Arabs sometimes seem to have a stronger sense of being part of an Arab nation than Europeans have of being European. No parallel therefore exists with the circumstances which led to the formation of the U.S.A., or the birth of Germany, Australia, Italy or the state of Switzerland. There is also no popular demand for the creation of a new European state. From the start, governments have been the pacemakers, and popular acceptance (rather than popular enthusiasm) has followed later. My own impression (a somewhat superficial one) of the reaction of younger people in Europe to the Community is one of indifferent acceptance. The Common Market is to them a commercial undertaking for which they can muster no great zeal. On the other hand they regard the crossing of frontiers for discussion, for work or study, as the most natural thing in the world. They have ceased to think in the nationalist terms that prevailed before the war. The Community is taken for granted and this in itself is a great gain.

There is therefore a contrast between, on the one hand, the absence of either popular demand or any of the historic ingredients for a new state, and, on the other, the pressures for international, not national, actions on a European plane arising out of several urgent and vital issues. I suspect that as a result the Community will emerge as an entity very much *sui generis*. It will have many of the attributes of a federation, and certainly a degree of centralized power that is inconsistent with either an association of states or a confederation; but the centralized powers will be kept as few as possible. There will be more residual power left in the hands of former nation states than most constitutional experts would regard as consistent with a classical federal model. Britain, France, Germany and the other Community members will not be reduced to the status of a Canadian province or of one of the United States of America.

Labour's policy of the cold shoulder towards Europe not only vitiates its policy towards some of the major issues of our time; what is even more serious is that a radical voice is not heard from Britain in the debate on the future development of the Community. Many social democrats in Europe struggle to make Community institutions the instrument of progressive social change. They receive no help or comfort from the Labour Party. The facts of international life may, as I have argued, force member states into giving the Community institutions more power; but only pressure from political parties can ensure that this power is democratically controlled. Yet, on issues like the budgetary powers of the European Parliament, which are crucial to the future of democracy in the Community, the Labour Party is silent. It is not even represented in the Parliament when this debate takes place. Without direct elections European Members of Parliament will neither be physically strong enough nor carry sufficient political authority to act as effective

M.P.s. Moreover, without direct elections it is only too likely that the Strasbourg Parliament will continue to shun the controversy that is the meat and drink of political debate and will do little more than express a preference for virtue and a bias against sin. Yet on this issue, too, the Labour Party remains silent, because within its own narrow horizons the European Parliament does not exist.

An insular party, like the Labour Party in its present guise, battling in close alliance with Enoch Powell to cling to the last inch of national sovereignty, cannot be regarded as a radical force. It is a tragedy that the pro-Europeans within it seem to regard the preservation of Party unity as more important than fighting boldly and publicly for the internationalism in which they believe. Since the vote on principle in favour of entry on October 28th, 1971, they have gone to ground. Before that vote the strong stand of the pro-Market M.P.s steadied the Party and prevented a full commitment to withdrawal. Since then the compliance of the same group for the sake of Party unity has allowed the outright opponents of British membership to set the tone. In time the pro-Europeans may be forced to realize that an anti-European Labour Party is incompatible with the ideals of social democracy.

9

THE CONSTITUTION

In Chapter 7 I indicated that the Labour Party's formal links with the unions could prove to be the cause of the decline of the Party as the main political force of the Left. Before I come to the reasons for this diagnosis, it becomes necessary to look closely at the nature of these links. They were created by the constitution of the Party and have helped to shape its character. What I regard as the Party's weakness, namely its constitution, is regarded by left-wingers, for symmetrically opposite reasons, as the Party's strength.

One of the central tenets of the current political credo of the left wing is that the decisions of Party Conference must be obeyed by Party leaders. This principle has been discovered by the left wing comparatively recently. It was elevated to its present eminence at about the time when the leadership of the biggest unions passed into left-wing hands. (It was at about the same time that some right-wingers suddenly realized that Conference had no right to dictate to M.P.s.) Left-wingers maintain that Conference must reign supreme because it is the expression of Party democracy—it is the annual assembly, in solemn session, of the Labour movement, representing the working class that is its base—the coming-together of the trade unions and their political allies, the constituency parties.

To understand the Labour Party one must look beyond the Party in Parliament and study its grass roots. The ordinary Party worker does not see himself (or herself) as a political private, duty-bound to carry out the officers' commands. He will probably be a reasonable individual, aware of his limitations, ready to accept that on a large number of issues his own knowledge is insufficient to make him the final arbiter of policy.

But he feels himself part of a movement in which democratic roots run deep, and he wants to know that when he has listened to the arguments, he, and others like him, will have some say in formulating the policy of his local party, which in turn will help to formulate the policy of the Labour Party as a whole. To become a Party worker means making sacrifices, being willing to knock on doors or address envelopes instead of going fishing or playing golf, spending time with the family or watching the telly. The Party worker is willing to make these sacrifices because he probably has some idea of the changes he wishes to see in society. He is not the type to believe in the monopoly of wisdom of an elite.

Many active Party workers (certainly in industrial constituencies like Lincoln) are also active trade unionists. Many people first become interested in the Labour Party through the trade union movement. They may have their first taste of political discussion at work, starting with concern about wage rates and proceeding naturally to a consideration of the inequalities of the class system in which 'they' (the employers) get all the perks and the working man the kicks. They will learn, in the hard school of experience, the need for solidarity if anything is to be accomplished. 'United we stand, divided we fall' is an old and respected trade union tradition, which enunciates a simple truth about life on the shop floor. Unlike the middle classes, who aim at improving their lot through individual effort and promotion, the trade unionist's hope of a higher standard of living depends largely on collective action. Individual conscience seems a luxury, possibly even a threat, although religious objections have, in practice, nearly always been respected. In general it is everyone's duty to accept majority decisions and to persuade others to do the same. Collective wisdom is respected because only collective action can succeed. At first, I was astonished to hear at Party Conference the readiness with which some trade union leaders argued, lawyer-like, for the brief handed to them by their union, even when their personal views were known to be the opposite of what they said. I recognize now the reason why they do so.

Three traditions therefore feature prominently in the Labour Party: a desire for Party democracy, whereby the movement should decide its own policy rather than accept it from its leaders; a strong link between experience in the trade union movement and work in the Party; and, finally, a readiness to submerge individual opinions in the majority decisions of the Party, together with a widespread expectation that others should do likewise.

This background helps to explain why the Labour Party shows a different approach to the question of loyalty in Party politics from that of the Conservative Party. Tories can be quite ruthless in persecuting those who oppose their Party on certain gut issues. I have already referred to Nigel Nicolson and Sir Anthony Nutting as two of those who might be reluctant to sign a testimonial to the tolerance of the Conservative Party. But when Tories err, their Party members do not accuse them of 'betraying the Party' so much as of betraying the country, or at least of showing that their basic judgment is not really sound. It is assumed that the Conservative Party represents the national interest, and one does not need to be an active Party worker to be a sound Conservative. Indeed, Conservatism is not a matter of politics at all; it is assumed to be the natural order of things.

Many people in the Labour Party, on the other hand, regard themselves as part of a movement rather than of just a party, a movement which is felt to be bigger than the individual. Socialism is more than just a set of principles; to many, especially the left wing, it is a cause to which men devote their lives and, like a religion, it has its martyrs. 'The people's flag is deepest red' because it is steeped in the blood of those who died for the cause. Cowards may flinch and traitors may sneer, but one day the workers will establish their Utopia. In this setting—which for the left wing has the strong emotional commitment of a religion, and where it is not meaningless to talk about 'the faith'—it is natural to use the words 'traitor to the movement' when someone prefers his own judgment to the collective wisdom of the movement as a whole, especially to the extent of being prepared to leave it.

The movement is a many-splendoured thing. It rumbles along (if movement is to be regarded as a literal description) through a variety of organizations. There are ward branches of constituency parties, local branches of trade unions, women's co-operative guilds, women's sections of constituency parties, branches of local Fabian societies and, in some constituencies, branches of the Young Socialists. Each may move resolutions, and these will finally wend their way through the local parties or national unions to Annual Conference. Certainly, at first sight, all the appearance of democracy is there—but the substance belies the appearance. When it comes to votes, under the constitution only one group really matters: the unions. Over four-fifths of the votes at the Annual Conference are the block votes of the big unions, because a union's vote depends on the number of its members who pay the political levy (in effect, those who do not contract out of the obligation to pay it); in the case of the Engineers or the Transport Workers, this gives them a block vote of over a million each. Neither the constituencies, which provide the active workers, nor the Parliamentary Labour Party, which provides the Party leadership but which has no vote, can outweigh the massed ranks of the industrial wing of the movement.

At first glance, it might seem surprising that the unions should so dominate the votes, since any trade unionist who wants to join the Party joins a constituency party which would represent him at Conference. Left-wingers, however, advance two arguments in defence of the block votes of the unions under the present constitution. The first is that the institutional links with the unions, the industrial wing of the movement, ground the Labour Party in what left-wingers regard as the reality of our society. The unions are the only alternative source of finance to the corporations which finance the Conservative Party, in a society where the conflict of interests is still basically that between management and unions. It is argued that the Constitution is a reflection of the fact that the Labour Party represents the section of society which is still the less well off, the working class. (I shall examine this argument more fully in the next chapter.)

The second line of defence is that the Constitution does in fact express the wishes of the Party effectively. This argument has a superficial plausibility and deserves careful examination.

It is true that whatever the theoretical objections to the form of the Constitution, the views of the majority of the constituency parties, as illustrated by the votes at Party Conference, do nowadays coincide with the votes of the large left-wing unions. When, for example, the vote against Britain's entry into the European Community on the terms negotiated was passed at the Conference of 1971 by a majority of five to one, analysis showed that this was a fair reflection of the votes in the constituency parties as well. Again, on domestic issues, the leaders of the Transport Workers and of the Engineers preach a doctrine of left-wing socialism after the Tribune mould; all the evidence suggests that most constituency activists, certainly since June 1970, espouse the same beliefs. In the days of the Bevanites it may have been the case that union block votes frustrated the wishes of the constituencies. Then, the constituency activists supported Bevan, while the trade union leaders were tough right-wingers determined to support the right-wing leadership of the Parliamentary Party. At that time Richard Crossman even argued that the Labour Party might be wise to re-examine its constitutional links with the trade unions. But today the two wings of the movement march militantly arm in arm.

The argument that this consonance of views makes the constitution democratic is of course without merit. A constitution must be democratic in form. If its form is defective, it does not become democratic merely because at a particular moment of time it expresses majority views. According to the above argument, a dictatorship which has popular support would be democratic. The Greek Colonels and Franco have both claimed to govern with popular support, and their claims may be justified. Both Hitler and Mussolini had popular support during most of their period in power. Stalin was popular in Russia. But dictatorships are not democracies because they do not provide for democratic forms of expression. Similarly, if the block votes of the trade unions reflect the views of the majority of the Party today, this does not in itself justify the Constitution unless the block votes themselves can be justified in democratic terms. This they cannot.

First, there is an element of double voting. Party members who are members of trade unions vote both through their constituency party and through their union. This is a parallel to the position inside the constituency parties themselves, where a trade union member can vote twice, as a member of a ward and as a member of an affiliated branch of his union. What is more, that part of the block vote to which double voting does not apply (the largest part of it) represents a phoney Party membership. It represents those who have not contracted out of paying the political levy to the Party. The reasons why people do not contract out are varied, but they do not necessarily signify a willingness to belong to the Labour Party. Many 'contracted-in' members of unions vote Conservative.

Next, those who are elected to the various policy-making bodies of the unions represented at the Labour Party Conference are not elected in the first place to determine the policy of the Labour Party. They are elected for a different purpose, namely to be that union's industrial representatives. Don Gossop, the District Secretary in Lincoln of the Amalgamated Union of Engineering Workers, and then a vice-chairman of the Lincoln Labour Party, was challenged during the Lincoln by-election about his support for a Communist candidate, Dixon, against a Labour Party candidate, in an election for the Executive Committee of his union. He defended himself on the grounds that union considerations were different from political considerations. He had not inquired, he explained somewhat unconvincingly, about Dixon's political affiliations. Other more moderate trade unionists have often told me that they would vote for the best *union* leader, because of his qualities as a union negotiator or as an industrial representative, even if he were a Communist. Communists can of course be good union negotiators. Will Paynter (now no longer a Communist Party member) and Arthur Horner were both able and responsible leaders of the Mineworkers' Union. But whether or not Communists can be good negotiators, those elected for their qualities as industrial representatives also vote under the Labour Party Constitution on resolutions which may decide the policies of the Labour Party. They may decide its foreign policy, or its attitude to housing, schools, building societies or defence. I do not believe that the trade unionists who voted for the election to office of Jack Jones or Hugh Scanlon (not, one should note, a high percentage of those qualified to vote) did so because they wanted them to determine the Labour Party's policy towards NATO or on nationalization or the Common Market. To leave the determination of Labour's policy to trade union leaders is about as democratic as allowing the elected representatives of a tenants' association to decide a local council's policy on museums.

Another fundamental flaw in the Constitution is that it makes Members of Parliament the servants of the Conference in a way which conflicts with their duties and responsibilities as M.P.s. Under the Constitution, a two-thirds majority for a particular policy at Party Conference makes that the official policy of the Labour Party. The Parliamentary Labour Party, it has been stated again and again, retains a discretion on questions of timing or tactics; but, these apart, it should accept the decisions of Conference. Mr Wilson has recently extended the official doctrine by claiming a power of veto for the Shadow Cabinet. He presumably bases this claim on the fact that the election manifesto must be drawn up jointly between the National Executive Committee and the Shadow Cabinet. A careful reading of the Constitution, however, suggests that the power of the Shadow Cabinet is no greater than that of the Parliamentary Party, namely a power over tactics and timing: the Shadow Cabinet has a say in the selection of those particular items out of the various policies of the Party which they feel should form part of the election manifesto because they can be implemented in a five-year programme. It would seem to be unconstitutional for the Shadow Cabinet, or for that matter the Parliamentary

Party, to proceed in a direction opposite to that laid down by Party Conference.

I have already argued in Chapter 1 (page 20) that the Constitution divorces power from responsibility; but it also ignores the fact that a Member of Parliament is accountable to the electors as much as to his Party. This issue lay at the heart of my arguments with the Lincoln Labour Party. By the nature of his trade, a Member of Parliament makes public statements and argues publicly that particular policies are right or wrong. He does so as an individual, not simply as a Party servant. He makes promises (probably far too many of them) at election time. If he is forced to renounce his views because he must obey Conference decisions, he destroys the credibility which politicians need. One can illustrate the dilemma of the parliamentarian by recalling the conflicting votes of Labour Party Conference in 1959, 1960 and 1961 on defence. One of the issues of the day was whether Britain should remain a member of NATO. If M.P.s had to obey Conference decisions, a Labour Member of Parliament would have had to argue in 1959 that NATO was the basis of our security; in 1960 that NATO was a danger to peace; and in 1961 he would once more be persuading his constituents that NATO was, after all, the basis of our security and not a danger to peace. At that stage, any of his constituents who were still listening might have felt justified in hurling rotten eggs.

Some consistency in the actions of Members of Parliament is not merely a question of ego, of preserving their self-respect or the good name of politicians. The validity of democratic choice is at stake. A vote for a political candidate is meaningful only if one knows what one is voting for—that is, if politicians mean what they say and vote in Parliament for what they believe in. If they vote as told, whatever their previous commitments, parliamentary elections become a charade and democracy becomes a lottery.

The position of a Member of Parliament is in any event a complex one. Most people agree that he should not simply act as lobby fodder for his Party. For the rest, they are somewhat confused. 'He should speak his mind,' 'He should stick to his guns and keep his commitments,' 'He should represent the views of his constituents,' are all sentiments which command a wide measure of acceptance. But these duties may conflict. He may speak his mind in an unpopular cause. He may feel that a commitment which he made was mistaken. What if popular opinion changes, as it sometimes does? And whose opinion must he represent? Does he owe a duty to represent the views of those who voted against him?

Democracy in Britain has never been a simple matter of making sure that parliamentary representatives reflect popular opinion at all times. Democracy is not synonymous with populism. Regular and frequent referenda or government by opinion polls are inconsistent with parliamentary government as we know it in Britain. Parliamentary democracy means the periodic competition of parties for public favour, to ensure that unpopular Governments can be overturned. It means consultation with those most directly affected by Government proposals. It means the rule of law and tolerance towards minorities. It also depends upon parties which enable people to vote for a programme of government; therefore it means that an M.P. must owe some loyalty to his Party as well as to the electorate. On the other hand, when an M.P. puts Party before the national interest, he breaks the trust placed in him by his constituents.

I believe that any sensible politician will obviously take the views of the public, and in particular of his constituents, into account. Likewise he will consider the sensibilities of his national Party and his local Party workers. But in the end he should make it clear what he believes in and what he will seek to promote. If the principles which he stands for are not acceptable, he should be ready to face rejection rather than change his stand. I do not suggest that he should never change his mind, only that he should not change his views for reasons of tactical or personal advantage. Equally, he would be foolhardy and unpractical if he was inflexible about every minor point of detail. Above all, a politician should remember that the Vicar of Bray was not the embodiment of political virtue.

Such considerations are not uppermost in the minds of delegates to Labour Party Conferences, any more than they prevailed with the Management Committee of the Lincoln Party. Conference feels that M.P.s must not give themselves airs. They were elected because Party workers worked for them. They should feel privileged to serve the Labour movement. They should accept the democratic verdict of the Conference in the manner in which trade union leaders accept the majority decisions of their unions and are then willing to speak for the union whatever their private views.

There is one further consequence of allowing no special role for the Parliamentary Party at the Conference (except allowing M.P.s to attend *ex officio* and speak): it leaves the Labour voter who is not a Party member without representation. The views of Labour voters and active Party workers do not necessarily coincide; indeed the evidence suggests that they may be a long way apart. To the activists in the Lincoln Labour Party, Conference was the supreme moment of the political year. They felt at home there. They met their political soul-mates. There is no doubt that they were far more in tune with the feelings of the majority of Conference delegates than were the Jenkinsite members of the Parliamentary Labour Party. Any comparison of the attendance at Tribune rallies and at the sedate, restrained and intellectual tea-gatherings of Socialist Commentary shows at once where the weight of numbers lies. Yet, as the Lincoln by-election demonstrated, those who feel most in tune with Conference are least in tune with popular feeling. M.P.s are, by and large, men and women of more moderate views than most of the constituency delegates or the leaders of the big unions, and much closer to the feeling of the average Labour voter. Elections to the Shadow Cabinet show that the members of the Parliamentary Labour Party choose a different group of leaders from those who top the poll in the constituency vote at Annual Conference. Tribunites dominate the National Executive Committee. They win only a minority of places on the Shadow Cabinet, even today when the Tribune Group in Parliament is stronger than it has been for a long time. The reason is not hard to find: M.P.s need to win elections and have to persuade the public; active Party workers do not.

The reform of this historical anachronism of a constitution poses an almost insuperable problem for the social democrats inside the Labour Party. It has been suggested from time to time that the votes of the constituency section should be given a greater influence and those of the trade unions should be reduced. Even if this reform were achieved—and it would need a voluntary abdication from power of the union leaders—it would provide little comfort for the social democrats. They are no more likely to win the support of most constituency delegates, who are always likely to be activists with predominantly left-wing leanings, than they are to win control of the biggest unions. What would do most to improve their position is a recognition of the need for greater independence for the Parliamentary Party. This, in turn, could best be promoted by altering the system of selecting M.P.s.

There is at the moment a kind of logic about the lack of recognition of the place of M.P.s under the Labour Party Constitution. Delegates to Conference from constituencies are appointed by the Management Committees of the local parties. These committees are of course the same bodies which select parliamentary candidates. In principle, a Member of Parliament (or parliamentary candidate) can be chosen by the local party also as the Conference delegate, and occasionally he is. If a Member of Parliament owes his position as M.P. to appointment by the same body which sends delegates to the Party's Conference and which could select him as a delegate, why should M.P.s need separate representation? Moreover, while M.P.s are selected in this way, is not the principle of their dependence on the Party organization established from the moment they become M.P.s?

In Chapter 2 of this book I have described the selection process. It need not involve many people. In many constituencies the Management Committee is smaller than it was in Lincoln and may consist of no more than thirty or forty delegates. Yet in 'safe seats' the body which selects the candidate also, in effect, chooses the Member of Parliament. Usually, in at least 400 out of a total of 630 constituencies, traditional Party loyalties prevail and the floating voter has no influence. Towns such as Southend or Bournemouth return Conservative M.P.s, and constituencies like Durham or Ashfield return Labour M.P.s—whatever the mood of national politics or the merit of individual candidates. In Southend or Durham the local parties are therefore the effective electorate. If this electorate consists of fewer than sixty people, it has a very narrow base.

The ideal answer lies in some form of Primary system, as in America. The aim would be to involve the maximum number of people in the selection of the candidate, yet at the same time to ensure that the power of money did not influence the result of a Primary campaign. The widest participation would be obtained by providing for a register of Party voters in each constituency, on the American model, and by giving all those who registered a right to choose that Party's candidate. Perhaps this would be too revolutionary a change for British politics. Making the selectorate (that is those with the right to choose the candidates) consist of all local Party members and not just of its governing body would be a reasonable compromise. As would-be contenders might well be numerous, the Management Committee—or perhaps the local Executive of the Party—must retain the power to draw up a short list. Those who are short-listed must then be given a chance to put their views before the selectorate. Public meetings would have to be arranged and perhaps interviews on local radio, and each candidate should be given a chance to circulate a statement to every member of the selectorate. All these activities would have to be financed from Party funds so that the wealth of a candidate (or his supporters) played no part. I should add that there is no reason why the procedure for re-adopting Members of Parliament before General Elections should not take exactly the same form. Parties should have the right to change their Members of Parliament, provided that the widest possible number of Party voters or Party members take part in the decision.

Whatever variations might be needed in this scheme, there is no doubt that a Primary system is quite compatible with the British Party system. Indeed, it would bring about a number of much-needed improvements. Caucus rule would become more difficult. A Member of Parliament would feel freer to resist attempts by his local officers or his Management Committee to influence his actions in Parliament. He would have more authority to speak within the Party, as someone selected by the widest possible Party group. Because its members would have a more democratic Party base, the Parliamentary Labour Party could legitimately claim to have a more influential voice within Conference that it has now, or, better still, a separate position inside the Party Constitution more independent of Conference. A Primary system would undoubtedly strengthen the social democratic wing of the Party, because, by its nature, a broader selectorate would favour those with moderate views. Above all, it would give the voter a more effective choice. Not unreasonably, the average voter who wants a Labour or Conservative Government now votes for the Party label rather than the man; it is, after all, the victory of a party which determines this kind of government. Instead he could help to choose the man as well as support the Party.

Desirable as this reform may be, it is unlikely that it will be accepted by the Labour movement. The movement is too conservative about its constitution. When I argued both with Labour Party colleagues and before the N.E.C. that ordinary members of the Party should be allowed to participate in a decision to dismiss a Member of Parliament, my arguments fell on deaf ears. Most of them seemed to feel that selection and dismissal alike could safely be left in the hands of Management Committees. They were not at all persuaded by the fact that, in the Conservative Party, both selection and dismissal, especially dismissal, involve far greater numbers of local association members. The present National Executive would also view with deep suspicion any reform which might strengthen the moderate elements in the Party.

Social democrats inside the Labour Party must recognize that there is no real prospect of change. They must live with the constitution. The best they can hope for is that enough people will be willing to ignore it.

10

THE CLASH OF INTERESTS

Most people who give a reason for voting Labour say that they do so because it is the Party of the working man, or the Party 'for people like us', by which they mean the working class. On the face of it, this explanation seems to confirm the analysis that politics in Britain are based on class and will continue to be so in the foreseeable future. In the last chapter, I mentioned that left-wingers defend the Constitution of the Labour Party on the grounds that the weight it gives to union votes reflects the basic class divisions of our society. The Labour Party Constitution ties the Party closely to the organization which speaks as the voice of the working class and which came into existence to protect its interests. Obviously the future of the Labour Party will depend to a large extent on the future role of the unions in our society and the likely evolution of class attitudes.

If anyone suggests that a conflict of interests may exist between the aims of a radical party and the activities of the trade unions, they are liable to be accused of union-bashing. Some liberal-minded people apply two standards: they tolerate anti-social behaviour by a minority of trade unionists (or, at most, regard it as a minor aberration), whereas they denounce similar behaviour by employers. In particular, in reaction to McCarthyism, they look askance at anyone who draws attention to Communist or Trotskyist influence within the trade union movement, because to them this smacks of a witch-hunt; yet connections with the National Front or Mosleyites must be rigorously exposed by every responsible citizen. I myself regard the undemocratic groups at either political extreme as equally dangerous. I also feel it does no service to the union movement to gloss over its weaknesses as if they do not exist. It is right to look at its functions as critically as one would look at the functions of employers' organizations or other interest groups.

Let me begin by asserting unequivocally that the trade union movement plays a valuable role in society. If it did not exist, wage-earners would be worse off than they are today. Unions not only protect the interests of their members; in many areas of industry they improve communications between management and employees. Their existence can help both sides of industry, as many employers confirm. Employers often welcome strong leadership from the shop floor (just as I have heard some union leaders complain that employers are sometimes not tough enough with some groups of shop-floor workers). For historical reasons, the organization of the unions in Britain is illogical and inefficient, with large unions spread across various industries and firms, often competing with one another for members among the same group of workers; but neither the unsatisfactory structure of unions nor the irresponsible action of militants is the main cause of industrial strife in Britain. The blame for bad industrial relations lies mainly with bad management. The unions are needed by society today and will be needed tomorrow.

To recognize the valuable contribution of the unions, however, is not to say that a party of the Left should necessarily reflect their views. It may be to the advantage of both if they were less closely linked. When the Labour Party formed the Government, it was inevitable that the unions did not always like what the Government was doing. At such times the formal links between the two, through the Party, either did not help or proved a positive embarrassment.

Again, it must be recognized that not all union activities automatically further the cause of social justice. It would be surprising if they did. After all, the unions represent a sectional interest group. It may be a large section of society that they represent; nevertheless what is good for a special interest group is not necessarily good for society as a whole.

My contention is that the very close identity which exists today between the political and industrial wing of the Labour movement prevents the Labour Party from formulating relevant and radical policies, not only for industrial reform but also for other kinds of social change. The Party has almost become the voice of some of the union leaders. Indeed, sometimes it acts like a minor member of the Trades Union Congress terrified of disciplinary action. Naturally, many of the social aims of union leaders are also the aims of the Labour Party. Both want a bigger share of the nation's wealth to go to pensioners; both rightly want to alter a social system in which property-millionaires appear by the dozen while countless thousands of people live in slums. A common belief about society is not, however, a guarantee that there will never be a clash of interests, and it is important to pinpoint the issues where such a clash occurs.

First, the Labour Party should unambiguously condemn the actions of a minority of militants which threatens liberty and democracy. Those who send their fellow-workers to Coventry for refusing to go on strike, or shout down opposition at meetings, or act as a stage-army of flying pickets to intimidate other workers who are carrying on their lawful tasks, are enemies of liberty or democracy, or both. Indeed, the leaders of the militants are often Trotskyites or Communists bent on destroying democracy as we know it. They bring discredit to the trade union movement as a whole and to the cause of conscience and reform. It is a disgrace that Labour leaders, with the honourable exception of Reg Prentice, seem to regard it as damaging to their relations with the unions to denounce such conduct.

More important, because it goes to the root of our economic and social ills, is the Labour Party's attitude to inflation. Apart from many other effects, inflation endangers full employment and redistributes wealth, mainly from poor to rich. Those who own property or land, or who have borrowed large sums of money at fixed rates of interest, become richer; those who live on fixed incomes, or whose incomes take time to adjust, become poorer. If inflation accelerates, the stability of our society may collapse. The outlook for Britain could be very ugly.

No one can blame inflation entirely on wage claims. Higher food prices throughout the world, higher interest rates, excessive demand, inadequate control of the money supply, may all contribute in different ways and at different times to the rise in prices. However, there is little room for reasonable doubt that a major factor causing inflation in Britain today is the rapid rise in incomes. If this were slowed down, then, after a time-lag, inflation would moderate. Some people refuse to acknowledge this, because it offends against deeply held political convictions about the rights of the working man, or because it conflicts with the purpose of their calling, if that is to negotiate for higher wages, or because they would like to see strict monetary discipline enforced instead. Nevertheless, those responsible for the conduct of affairs are compelled, one after the other, as a central part of their policy against inflation, to look at ways of controlling the rise in incomes. The Conservatives in Britain, like the Republicans in the United States before them, began by refusing to consider statutory controls over incomes. They have been forced to eat their words. I personally find it hard to see how Britain can go back to a free-for-all and avoid a statutory framework for regulating wage claims.

Just when the need for statutory controls over prices and incomes has been conceded by the champions of *laissez-faire*, the Labour Party puts forward a policy for statutory controls of prices but not of incomes. This is like calling for a reduction in the crime rate while abolishing the police.

The explanation is that consultation with the unions revealed, not unexpectedly, that they would not accept a statutory framework. The unions will not do so on principle, because their whole *raison d'être* is to promote free collective bargaining. Any regulation of the maximum increase in wages eliminates part of the purpose for which unions exist. Yet it is clear that in present circumstances the operation of an incomes policy that is voluntary is a pipedream. Some unions would not give their consent; others would not implement a general agreement, even if they had signed it. Those who were willing both to sign an agreement and to keep it would suffer from the actions of the rest. A voluntary agreement must be observed by all to be effective. Either we have no incomes policy of any kind, or we must accept one based on statutory powers. By rejecting the idea of a statutory policy, the Labour Party is left with the choice between inflation and massive unemployment.

Apart from the control of inflation, a statutory framework for regulating collective bargaining also seems to offer the best hope of a fairer structure for wages.

Something has gone wrong with the way different wage rates are determined. This is clear from the nature of many strikes. Originally a strike was designed to force the employers' hand by blocking his profits. Today some strikes are caused by fellow workers over the demarcation of jobs, or over questions of union recognition. Others, often those with the most widespread effects, are strikes against the Government by public employees or workers in nationalized industries. However, they can only influence the Government indirectly. Their direct impact is on the public, on unfortunate railway travellers or hospital patients who have no responsibility for, or power over, levels of pay. Not all the blame for the inconvenience or suffering caused to innocent outsiders can be placed on those who go on strike. They feel (often with justice but sometimes without – engine drivers are paid more than the national average wage) that they have no other way of improving an unfairly low level of wages. Sometimes the wages of some workers have fallen behind precisely because the suffering which a strike would cause has made them reluctant to use the strike weapon, although other workers have not hesitated to use their bargaining power. The moral is, to my mind, plain: a free-for-all, the rule of the strongest, produces injustice. To achieve a wage structure which is less unjust a statutory policy for incomes is essential.

However, there are some who question whether an incomes policy can ever lead to the establishment of a fairer wage structure, because fairness is too subjective a criterion. Indeed, one has to concede that there is no ideal pattern of levels of pay. There is no universal agreement about the value of different jobs in terms of pay. On the other hand, you *can* say that a system in which two people do the same job and are paid differently is *un*fair, or that some differentials are unfairly large, or that some wage levels are too low by any standard. To eliminate injustice is often a practical aim, even if justice is an elusive concept.

It has also been argued that an incomes policy cannot be used to reduce the gaps that now exist between different levels of pay, because differentials are too firmly entrenched. They have, it is argued, altered very little over the last decade, whether or not an incomes policy was in force. If the wages of the lowest-paid are raised by more than the average, other wage increases will also be larger than they otherwise might have been, since differentials are bound to be restored in time.

There can be no conclusive answer to the argument, largely because our experience with incomes policies has so far been limited. The incomes policy introduced by the Labour Government in 1965 was relaxed when the 1970 election approached. It has to be conceded that many people keep a close watch on the wage levels of those with whom they have always compared themselves. They are as worried about the decline of their relative position as they are about the pay itself. To force them to accept a worse position than they are used to is as difficult as trying to keep all wage increases within a certain limit. To narrow differentials as well as fight inflation is therefore a task made doubly difficult.

These obstacles should make Governments modest in their aims. Probably, they can hope to hold the line within a new structure of relative levels of pay only if they have strong public support. There would have to be a widespread feeling that certain anomalies of pay were intolerable or that a particular group of workers, like hospital workers, needed a special boost. Even then, a Government could make an exception for one group of workers only if it was clear that a rash of further exceptions could be prevented. The alternative policy, put forward by those who believe that an incomes policy cannot be used to promote social justice, is to use fiscal means. Tax credits might help the lowest paid, but I am not sure how far increasing the marginal rate of tax more steeply on higher incomes would promote redistribution. Past experience is discouraging.

There is one other industrial issue where radical policies may be prejudiced by the need to gain trade union consent—industrial democracy. The unions favour the creation of two-tier boards for companies: one to be an executive board, the other a supervisory board. The first board would consist of managers; the second would take strategic decisions about matters such as take-overs and large-scale closures. On the second board, half the representatives would be nominated by the unions, and half by the shareholders. With some modifications—whereby employees and shareholders take one-third each of the seats on the supervisory board and nominate the last third jointly—I believe that this scheme has merit and deserves full discussion. However, whatever the merits of such a scheme, if people are to share in determining the conditions of work in the factories or offices they work in, representation by their union on a distant board is no adequate solution. They need more direct opportunities for exercising influence. Employees in a factory will need some sort of elected body to speak for them, and one which is elected by all employees irrespective of their union affiliation. If this body is to share in decisions about the conditions of the place of work, or the methods of working or training, or questions of discipline, it must be responsible solely to employees. It cannot consist of the representatives of rival unions. The very fact that unions in Britain are not industrial unions, but craft unions spread horizontally throughout industry, makes it hard to integrate them with what must be a vertical institution entirely concerned with each place of work. It is not surprising that the unions have shown no enthusiasm for such a potentially powerful rival.

The debate about industrial democracy has only just started. Perhaps it will emerge that such radical solutions are unworkable. But a Labour Party which cannot act independently of the unions is unlikely to advocate the more radical approach.

So far I have suggested that the constitutional ties between the Labour Party and the unions will prove an embarrassment to Labour because they inhibit the formulation of radical policies for inflation or a fairer wages structure, and perhaps even for industrial relations. I foresee two other developments which will work against the party. First, I expect a shift in the course of time away from the present obsession of all Governments with the growth of the Gross National Product. This will, I believe, be accompanied by the greater concern of society with the rights of the consumer rather than with the interests of the producer. Secondly, I expect there will be wider recognition of the dangers of centralization, of the advantages of variety, and of the need for human institutions to be reduced in scale.

Let me start with the dispute about economic growth. The argument that there are physical limits to the present rate of economic growth of the industrial nations is not a popular one with politicians, businessmen and economists. Most politicians and businessmen refuse to consider it at all. As the argument leads to unpalatable conclusions, they feel it must be false. The conclusions are unpalatable, because the creation of more wealth is regarded as self-evidently beneficial to mankind. It can abolish poverty. It enables Governments to plan for increased public spending on social ends without increased taxation. With good management, more wealth can also pay for the measures required to clean up our rivers, to make our cities more beautiful, to clean the atmosphere and to prevent the pollution of the sea. It provides for progress without tears. Economic stagnation instead of growth means that the poor can be helped only by taking from the rich (and the not so very rich). It means that social services can be improved only by using money obtained by extra taxation. It is also feared that people will not invest in industry in a capitalist economy unless the economy is growing. No wonder that politicians and businessmen regard the need for continued economic growth as axiomatic.

The argument that economic growth must be limited is based on three main propositions: first, that resources are finite and will some day become exhausted; second, that the economic growth of industrial nations disturbs the balance of nature and may even threaten the survival of mankind; third, that the consequences of economic growth will reduce the quality of life.

The first two propositions are obviously more fundamental than the third, for if unlimited economic growth is not possible, the question of whether it is desirable does not arise.

It should be noted that it is only the third proposition that politicians are disposed to challenge. Economists, however, have strongly disputed both the first and the second. They confidently assert that a combination of the price mechanism and new technology will confound the prophecies of doom. The price mechanism will automatically cause the substitution of resources which are in plentiful supply for those which are running short. Technology will ensure that alternative methods of supply will be developed that are not ecologically harmful, and that we will find more economical ways of using existing resources. Any shortage of energy, for instance, will be overcome in due course by using solar energy, or energy from nuclear fusion. In one way or another, technology and the price mechanism, the two saviours of economic man, will make everything come out all right in the end. As for pollution, if technology can send men to the moon, it can restore Lake Erie or make the seas around Japan once more clean enough for men to eat the fish that swim in them.

I must confess to some scepticism, and at the very least agnosticism, about the confident assertions made by the economists. First, no precedents apply. The huge increase in the world's industrial production is such a recent phenomenon that one must be allowed some doubts about whether all possible problems can always be solved. We meet increasing evidence—from the fall-out effects of H-bomb tests to thalidomide babies—that not all the consequences of technological developments were foreseen or foreseeable. Man has not previously been a disturbing force in nature on the present scale, and it is some cause for worry if he is not quite sure what he is about. Next, it seems to me almost inconceivable that even the most ingenious and sophisticated technology would enable the whole world, say at a population level of 7,000 million, to enjoy the standard of living of the United States today, let alone the United States of tomorrow. Again, if one understands the concept of exponential growth, it is hard to imagine how the developed world can go on indefinitely doubling its standard of living every twenty to thirty years (every five years in Japan).* Yet if either of the last two doubts are justified, then the case that economic growth is limited must be accepted. The question that remains is how, and when, the present pattern of industrial development will change.

The Japanese, whose economy has shown the fastest rate of growth, may be the first people to have to face the possible implications of their own rapid expansion. A recent report prepared by the Study Group for Industrial Planning (a private organization of thirty-one well-known businessmen and academic economists) warned that if present trends (which have now been fairly constant for over a decade) are projected, then Japan will need to import half the world's production of raw materials and half its annual production of oil by 1985. Drastic measures should, they say, be taken to reduce the growth rate. Some industries should be shut down altogether; others should freeze their production. If Japan does not plan ahead, dislocation will be sudden and disastrous. The recommendations of the report, it should be noted, are in complete contrast to the policies of the Tanaka Government.

Gloomy forecasts about the future of economic growth could be false. The scientific community, who almost without exception assume it cannot continue, may be profoundly mistaken, and the economists may be right. It would be easier to assess their conflicting judgments if they were more prepared to study each others' arguments. What seems unwise is to assume that there is no risk that the economists may be wrong. Sometimes, if the possible consequences are disastrous, Governments do take note of risks that are very small. There is less than a 1 per cent chance of the Thames overflowing in any one year. But the

* Perhaps the best example of exponential (or geometric or logarithmic) growth is that of the young man who persuaded his employer to pay him one penny on the first day, two pennies on the second, four on the third and so on. Each day his pay was to double until the end of the month. On the twenty-fifth day his pay amounted to over £167,000. Had the employer stayed in business he would have had to pay out more than £10 million for the month.

magnitude of the disaster to London if it happened would be so great that large sums were spent on raising the height of the river banks. If the developed world should have to face a major ecological crisis within a few generations, Governments should not proceed with blind indifference to the risks involved in their present course. They must act as trustees for future generations. Above all, politicians should think on a different time scale—not just in terms of the next week (which we are told is a long time in politics), nor just the period until the next election, but in terms of generations.

It would, in my view, be profoundly mistaken to react to the arguments in favour of limitations on economic growth by seeking an immediate end to all expansion. It would be impossible for a country like Britain to follow such a policy on her own. Nor would it be a sensible strategy for other developed nations. Not all technological progress damages our environment or wastes resources. Much of it can improve the former and preserve the latter. We need, instead, to frame our industrial and fiscal policies in such a way that good technology is encouraged and bad technology penalized. We also need to seek a different standard by which to measure national progress than the concept of the Gross National Product. This concept is a useful tool for economists. It measures the real (as opposed to inflationary) increase in a nation's incomes and expenditures. It does not claim to measure well-being. If doctors' bills increase because there is more illness, and laundry bills increase because there is more dirt, if the cost of travelling to work increases because people live farther from their work place, G.N.P. goes up. Hence the feeling so many people express that, although their income has risen (even in real terms), they are no better off. G.N.P. should cease to be the standard by which we judge international success.

In any event, it is likely that a different attitude towards the value of economic growth will emerge almost naturally, without the need for a mass conversion of Economic Ministers to the doctrines of Mishan, Meadows, Commoner or Ehrlich. Attitudes are already changing in a way which may place ever larger obstacles in the path of growth. Even from Germany and France, where the factory-workers are supposed to be models of applied industriousness, complaints are heard that the 'work ethic' is weakening. People value leisure more. Perhaps we shall yet see the export to Europe of the British tea-break. Environmental lobbies throughout the world are beginning to interfere with the expansionist plans of industry and commerce. In Britain, Canvey Island, an area already suffering from a plague of oil refineries, is determined to resist another one. But where will people accept new refineries? Forces resisting new airports, wherever they are planned, grow stronger every year. The same is true of opposition to the building of new roads. The public demands quieter aircraft, quieter motor-cars and cleaner ones too. Lorries are beginning to be regarded as the destroyers of civilized life, and motor transport will be increasingly restricted in towns and perhaps even in national parks. Less than five years ago, our environment was a subject of interest only to cranks and minor pressure groups. Today it features as one of the foremost political issues of our time.

The effect which these pressures will have is not easy to forecast. I myself guess that they will postpone or prevent certain kinds of economic development. Fewer urban motorways will be built, perhaps even fewer airports. The shortage of fuel supplies may be aggravated because of campaigns against the building of nuclear power-stations (the environment lobby in the United States has already delayed the building of the Alaska pipeline). Industrial costs will increase because of ever more stringent controls against social and physical pollution. The gradual shift from manufacturing to service industries will be accelerated. Political parties will be made to formulate their aims more in terms of non-material values, and less in terms of the maximization of G.N.P. In sum, if the society of tomorrow abandons our present obsession with economic growth it will be less dominated by the producers whose interests have so far been allowed to rule our lives. Prime consideration will be given to the social values of what is produced, to the effects on others of the operations of the manufacturers and to the preservation of scarce resources. There will be no production for production's sake. The ethos of our society will alter.

At first sight, such a change is wholly in line with socialist thinking, since service, not profit, has always been a battle-cry of socialism. It depends, however, on the way socialism is interpreted. If a socialist party is mainly a party of organized labour and the working class, its membership will diminish: as the number of people working in services grows, the number of those who identify with a working-class party decreases. Next, as redistribution of income will increasingly entail making the better-off worse off, the need to restrain free collective bargaining will become greater. Both of these developments will prejudice the prospects of a party which regards itself as based on the working class or which acts as the voice of unions who cannot officially accept restraints on their freedom to bargain.

Lastly, I believe that we shall also experience a reaction against centralization and giantism which conflicts with Labour's present proposals for public ownership.

It is illuminating to start a discussion about the merits of centralization or devolution with a parallel from nature. The more we learn about nature, the more we learn that the survival of life depends on balance and variety. Indeed, one of the most convincing arguments advanced by the ecologists about the dangers of industrial civilization to the survival of man is that man is a simplifying force who upsets the balance and variety of nature by his industrial activities. There is clear evidence that society, too, becomes more vulnerable as it becomes more centralized, as it becomes more dependent on specialist activities or special new materials, as cities and international corporations grow and grow. The go-slow of the power workers in 1971 showed how unwise it was for everyone to be dependent on centrally generated electricity. A small number of men nearly brought all industry in Britain to a standstill. Many hospitals have since installed their own electricity. Shortage of a vital metal can threaten an industry, as was found when there was a strike in a Canadian nickel mine. A few strikes in a small components factory can halt the motor industry. Two car bombs in London on March 8th, 1973, brought chaos to traffic in central London. The failure of one small cog can halt a very large and complex machine.

It has already been mentioned that the size and importance of large companies is increasing. This is part of a trend towards centralization that will need to be reversed. It should be the aim of radical politicians to break up the largest concentrations of power and not to increase them. We should seek to reform our technology in the direction of smallness and simplicity. Nothing could therefore be more mistaken than the doctrinaire proposal, put forward by the Labour Party, to create a monster National Enterprise Board, to control, and further centralize, the biggest companies in Britain. The Labour Party argues, in so far as its proposals are arguable at all, that centralization under public ownership is tolerable where centralization under private ownership is not, because public ownership means democratic control and ensures that industry serves the needs of society. Their plans ignore the dangers of centralization, and are blind to the lessons of experience.

First, a National Enterprise Board would be enormously powerful. Its purpose would be to direct the investment plans and the strategic decisions of a string of giant companies, whether they be twenty-five, twenty or ten. If the Board does not act as a rubber stamp for the plans for its subsidiary managers, it must develop a large staff, many times larger than the headquarters of the largest multi-national corporation. Presumably it would seek to increase efficiency and reduce costs by rationalizing and centralizing sources of supply, and thus it would increase the interdependence of the various parts of its empire. It would thereby reduce variety rather than increase it. The result would be to make British industry more vulnerable. An industrial dispute which is now confined to one firm, like that at British Leyland Motors (which might well be a candidate for takeover by the N.E.B.), would in future be more likely to involve other companies as well. Bad decisions of management now affect one firm; bad management by the Board could affect the major part of British industry. Whether centralization comes about under public or private ownership, vulnerability is increased.

Secondly, centralization can be a denial of liberty. An important part of freedom is the right to change one's job. There may be a limited number of posts that a person with special skills can fill. If there are several firms who are possible employers, he can change from one to the other. He retains the freedom to offend his superiors. But the N.E.B. would reduce opportunities of alternative employment. Independence would suffer and independence is a cornerstone of liberty.

Thirdly, how can Ministers, or Civil Servants, or Parliament, control such a body as the N.E.B.? During the period of the last Labour Government I often heard complaints from fellow Ministers that the Government had more control over private firms and received more co-operation from private industry than it had over, or received from, parts of the public sector. Pitched battles had sometimes to be fought against the war-lord of some vast public corporation. If the Government created a National Enterprise Board, a clash between Ministers and the head of the N.E.B. would compare with past conflicts as the battle of Waterloo does with the Gunfight at the O.K. Corral. I would be reluctant to bet on the representatives of democracy being the victors. The N.E.B. would carry the heavier guns. It would be the largest and most powerful industrial institution in the Western world.

At the beginning of this book, I argued that Hugh Gaitskell was right in 1959 to question Clause 4 of the Labour Party Constitution which made public ownership the basic principle of the Party's philosophy. The recrudescence of the debate about public ownership has vindicated his judgment.

Rational discussion of public ownership is confused by the dogmatism of Left and Right. Of course, it is proper that the Government should intervene to change 'the ugly and unacceptable face of capitalism'. The unrestrained pursuit of profitability and the uncontrolled competition of the market can wreck plans for a more responsible society and greater social justice. Public ownership has a part to play because it can ensure that social aims prevail. It is wrong, however, to suppose that the only way to make firms socially accountable is to nationalize them. Nationalization, because it reduces the number of firms, leaves less room for experiment and variety and change. The organization of industry must be as varied as we can make it. Some of it should be publicly owned, some municipally owned; there should be co-operatives, and companies whose profits are distributed by trustees for charitable purposes; there should be public and private companies and family firms. Variety is more important to human beings than efficiency.

When in doubt we should favour the small. Indeed, our guiding principle should be 'small is beautiful', that variety provides for independence, and that independence provides greater security and freedom for society as a whole.

11

THE FUTURE OF THE LEFT

THE LABOUR PARTY

In Part II of this book, I have discussed the Labour Party, its attitudes to Europe, its constitutional links with the unions and the way in which these links prejudice its radicalism. On the fate of the Labour Party depend both the future of the Liberal Party and the chances of realignment out of which a new Social Democratic Party might emerge.

There is often talk about a third force in the mid-term between General Elections. It starts most often when the Government is Conservative and unpopular, and the Opposition is Labour and split—most often, therefore, when a Labour Opposition is unable to make capital out of the Government's unpopularity. It subsides when the Labour Party succeeds in appearing to be able to form a viable alternative Government. When I became a Member of Parliament in 1962, the fortunes of the Labour Opposition were on the upward turn. Jo Grimond, then Leader of the Liberals, had been campaigning for a realignment of the Left—in effect for a social democratic party. Woodrow Wyatt, then M.P. for Bosworth, was calling for a Lib–Lab pact. The famous by-election at Orpington fired the hopes of the Liberals. But, instead of a Liberal revival, there followed a series of by-election successes for the Labour Party, from 1962–4, which squashed all talk of revival and banished all prospects of a Lib–Lab pact. By contrast, there is no sign in 1973 that the fortunes of the Labour Party are about to change. The Liberals have won a string of by-elections, and in the present political climate they are poised to win almost any seat that falls vacant. The Labour Party is in disarray. It is badly led; it is unable or unwilling to dissociate itself from the militant policy of left-wing union leaders; its left wing is dominant. It does not look like a viable alternative Government.

Since 1970, Labour's record in Opposition has been a poor one. For the first year the Party was largely absorbed in a fight against the Industrial Relations Bill, in which its attitude towards the Bill was as negative as its tactics were inept.*

The second year of Opposition was spent on internal quarrels about the Common Market. It was not until the third year that the Labour Party started to look seriously at constructive policies. A host of study groups reported, and plans were duly unveiled for massive extensions of nationalization, as well as for a series of desirable reforms which would cost over £5,000 million a year more than the plans of the present Government. The extra cost, it is claimed, will be financed largely from faster economic growth. Harold Wilson has described the programme as the best he has yet seen. In fact it represents a triumph of hope over experience. It seems as if the Party, frustrated by the moderate achievements of the last Labour Government, has decided to overcome the disappointments of the past by promising more in the future than it has ever promised before.

This combination of lack of realism and left-wing socialism, which the Labour Party now offers to the public, seems to provide a better chance today for the emergence of a possible third force than at any time since the war. But in fact, according to several opinion polls, the Liberals, who represent the third force, are still taking more votes from the Conservatives than from Labour. Why, then, do people speculate about the future of the Left? Why, today, does no one wonder about the future of the Right? The answer is, I think, that the Conservative Party is by its nature a more durable institution than either the Liberal or the Labour Parties. Sooner or later, the Conservatives will make up at least some of their lost support.

* The opposition to the Bill ended with one of the most futile demonstrations of recent parliamentary history. At Report Stage we voted against every new clause and amendment proposed by the Government (after a guillotine motion had cut short the debate). We even voted against amendments which were made at Labour's request. This involved marching through the lobbies continuously without argument for well over twelve hours. It was gesture politics at its worst. Trade unionists, for whose benefit the whole operation was staged, failed to notice.

Conservatism will last because it is human nature to dislike change. The Conservatives need no ideology (although when they are foolish they adopt one), and paradoxically this makes the Tory Party more adaptable when change is forced on it. The danger with ideologies is that, even if they are relevant when they are formulated, they can set fast and become outdated. This is especially likely to happen when means are confused with ends. (Nationalization was originally a *means* towards a better society; the left wing now regards it as an *end*.) To the non-ideological Tories, a change of front needs no justification, and they will preach one day that industry must stand on its own two feet, and the next day they will arrange, without as much as a by-your-leave, that it should stand on the tax-payers' feet. Only right-wing Tories need a creed and crave consistency. By contrast, those on the Left who are dissatisfied with society, who feel offended by its injustices and who seek major changes in its structure, almost inevitably conceive an ideal – hence their need for an ideology. It is also inevitable that people who wish to construct an ideal society will set their hopes too high. They may become cynical when their hopes are disappointed.

A more limited approach can be more rewarding. Egalitarianism, for instance, sounds drab; it connotes uniformity and levelling down, and most people do not like equality anyway. On the other hand, it makes sense and seems right and fair that we should end some of the offensive *in*equalities we see around us. People should not be allowed to make large fortunes out of land speculation while others live in slums. They should not be allowed to get rich by avoiding the taxes which the rest of us pay, while others live in poverty. The unpopularity of the Conservatives is partly caused by a strong sense that they have promoted unfairness; for example in the heady days after 1970, when they first won back power, they proceeded to help their friends, the rich, by handsome tax concessions. (Among other things, they allowed tax relief on overdrafts and personal loans, greatly reduced the tax on unearned income, and restored the separate taxation of certain kinds of children's income.)

Again, when it comes to happiness the same, negative, approach is more realistic. The greatest happiness of the greatest number was always too vague an objective, even before Professor Rawls showed that it might conflict with social justice. It makes sense, on the other hand, to fight to minimize misery. We can all recognize misery when we see it. We do not, most of us, know how we can promote happiness.

The fact that parties of the Left seek an ideology puts them in greater danger from doctrinal disputes. Hence the greater frequency of splits on the Left than on the Right. Indeed the farther Left, the more prevalent are arguments about the finer points of ideology, such as, for example, about how many nationalized companies can dance on the point of a needle. (The most violent arguments of all take place among Communists, International Marxists, International Socialists and various groups of Trotskyites.) It is on the Left that the future is uncertain, rather than on the Right, partly because the main party of the Left is at present more obsessed with ideological disputes than with providing practical answers to current problems.

I believe therefore that the Labour Party will look like a viable alternative Government again only if it has a new leader and if the views of the social democrats prevail. On this question the future shape of the politics of the Left depends.

At first sight the social democrats would seem to have a chance. The Leader of the Party is chosen by the Parliamentary Party and, as already mentioned, this is more moderate in complexion than either the constituency section of Conference or the leadership of the largest unions. The balance within the Parliamentary Party is held by the centre, which has not in the past wanted to identify too closely with either the Tribunites or the social democrats. If Labour loses the next election (I shall come presently to what may happen if it wins), why should not the Parliamentary Party revolt against the false prophets on the left wing who have led it to defeat? Harold Wilson's position would be in question. Would the Party not choose a leader with the greatest appeal to the floating voter? Would he not inevitably be a moderate social democrat?

Unfortunately, the Parliamentary Party does not constitute the Labour Party, or even an independent unit within it, and it is inevitable that in choosing a leader the ordinary Labour M.P. will look not only at a leader's appeal to the public, but also at his position in the Party. In the past, as was shown by the history of Hugh Gaitskell's struggles, not even the social democrats have been able to ignore Party Conference when the Party is in Opposition.* It is regarded as a truism in politics (perhaps wrongly) that popular appeal will not win votes unless it is backed by Party organization. Party workers must be prepared to go out on the doorstep. Further, the Labour Party organization depends on special trade union donations, as well as on union affiliation fees. It is unthinkable, therefore, to many Labour M.P.s that the Parliamentary Party should cock a snook at the constituency workers and the big unions alike, and select a leader whom the other sections of the Party would regard as unacceptable. The Parliamentary Party might refuse to choose the same leader as the Conference would choose, but they would hesitate long before choosing someone who might cause conflict.

It must also be remembered that, not unnaturally, Members of Parliament want to remain M.P.s. In the last resort, an irate Conference, which felt that M.P.s had let them down, could urge constituency parties to reconsider the adoption of those who flouted its wishes. In fact, it was the reports that Labour M.P.s were planning to ignore the Conference vote against Europe in 1971 which led Ian Mikardo, at a Tribune rally that week, to remind delegates that the remedy lay in their own hands—they were the ones who adopted M.P.s. Perhaps it is unlikely that there will be other Lincolns. But the threat of disownment can bring many M.P.s into line. Not all would be willing to fight back, or would be confident of long-term survival if they did.

Finally, many M.P.s are constitutionalists, who feel that they must always abide by the Constitution. They have lived with it for a long time and are less ready to criticize its forms than is a

* See Chapter 1, page 22.

constitutional lawyer analysing its claim to democratic justification.

For the social democrats to gain control of the Party is not, then, simply a matter of counting the heads of moderate M.P.s, and assuming that they will vote for a moderate leader. Somehow the social democrats must neutralize Conference. But the chances of them doing so seem slight. Inevitably, a large proportion of constituency delegates consists of the most dedicated Party workers. As I found at Lincoln, many of these would rather lose elections than compromise their view of socialism. The reaction of the Lincoln Party to its own defeat may foreshadow the likely reaction of other constituency militants. In their annual report, published a month after their defeat in the by-election of 1973, the Lincoln Party claimed that they had never been 'stronger or more united'. To them, purity of the faith equals strength. In any event, if Labour loses the next General Election, Party members will be told by Foot and Heffer and other leading figures of the Tribune Group that the Party failed, not because the left-wing message was not palatable to the public, but because the message was muted. They will blame the moderates for having attacked nationalization. No doubt they will argue that, if only Harold Wilson had not announced that he and the Shadow Cabinet would veto plans to nationalize twenty-five companies because he believed the plans would lose votes, there would have been a clear socialist alternative to the Tories. Party workers would have worked harder on the doorsteps. The working class in their masses would have streamed into the polling-booths to vote Labour.

The chance of the social democrats capturing control of the unions is no better. There is no sign that the possible successors of Jack Jones or Hugh Scanlon are less left-wing. The executive committees and the wider policy-making bodies of the Transport Workers and Engineering Unions have shown themselves no less militant on industrial issues than their leaders. The engineers recently voted unanimously for a large extension of nationalization and carried, by a small majority, a motion that there should be no compensation. In seats where Labour candidates who are sponsored by these unions have recently been adopted, they have nearly all been left-wing socialists.

The balance of power within the Party was different in 1960 and 1961, when Hugh Gaitskell, helped by the Campaign for Democratic Socialism, won back the support of Conference against left-wing neutralists. The power within the unions was then evenly balanced, with a right-winger, Bill Carron, holding the presidency of the Engineering Union. The National Executive of the Party was then dominated by Gaitskell's friends, whereas it is now controlled by the left wing. Hugh Gaitskell himself was prepared to fight for his principles, even if it meant a split within the Party, whereas Harold Wilson sees his main task as keeping the Party together.

My conclusion is that if the Labour Party is defeated at the next General Election, and if the Leader of the Party is then changed, either there will be a move farther to the Left, or a leader will be elected who is middle-of-the-road in Party terms, who makes moderate speeches but who tolerates power being held effectively by the left wing.

If the Parliamentary Party wants a leader to represent the social democrats it will have to issue a unilateral declaration of independence. This would be an illegal and unconstitutional act. It would require boldness and determination. The leader would have to be ready to defy both Conference and the National Executive Committee, and to assert the independence of the Parliamentary Party from the decisions of both. No doubt, in time, he would have to negotiate a settlement, a return to legality. He would have to throw some sops to the Cerberus of Conference—say, the nationalization of the odd bank or insurance company—but he would be able to extract concessions as well as make them.

Unfortunately there is little chance of such a declaration of independence. It would frighten the centre as much as it would appal the left wing. If Labour M.P.s nurture any rebellious thoughts of independence, they have concealed them well. Even the pro-Marketeers have shown little zest for battle since October 1971. The bulk of the Parliamentary Party seems to regard a spurious unity as a prize more valuable than electoral appeal. They would have to undergo a sea-change to dare to show defiance of Conference.

The picture alters entirely if Labour wins the election. This could happen if the inexorable rise in prices goes on and if, as is possible, there is a collapse of the economic policy of the Conservative Government. The Government may then lose, whatever the state of the Opposition.

The management of the economy by the present Conservative Government has been bold to the point of recklessness. Floating the pound was a defensible measure to avoid the kind of battle to save the parity of the pound which the Labour Government fought, mistakenly, between 1964 and the end of 1967. However, the problem of the balance of payments does not disappear because the pound is floating. It is unwise of the Government to float the pound while maintaining an uncontrolled economic expansion that attracts imports almost irrespective of their cost. As predicted by several economists early in 1972, a huge surplus on the balance of payments has turned into a huge deficit.* Consequently, the pound has sunk like a stone. The cost of imports has continually increased and inflation has been made worse. It is possible that the prices of raw materials may collapse, which would lower the cost of imports and rescue the Government's economic policy. But, at the time of writing, it appears that the Government may have to make a drastic change of course which might prejudice the chances of the Conservatives winning the next election.

If Labour wins, then it is likely to do so when economic conditions are adverse. Inflation will be running at a high rate. Economic expansion either will have been curbed, or will need to be curbed to redress the balance of payments. Uncertainty will be created by Labour's attitude to Europe and its plans for public ownership, which will lead to movements of capital out of Britain. In some respects the position will be the same as in

* See the report 'The Management of the Economy', prepared by the Department of Applied Economics in Cambridge for the General Sub-Committee of the Expenditure Committee, published in the *7th Report of the Expenditure Committee, Session 1971–1972*.

1964, when the Conservatives left the new Labour Government a legacy of a large deficit in overseas trade. In other respects it will be worse: the rate of inflation will be higher and the policies of the Labour Party are less appropriate to the management of the nation's economy.

In such circumstances, no crystal ball is needed to forecast a split within the new Labour Government between realists and left-wingers, and a conflict between the Government and the Labour rank and file. Within months an almost draconian incomes policy would be needed, despite previous solemn undertakings to avoid statutory controls. Wide-ranging social reforms, so liberally promised, would have to be postponed; so would plans for a large extension of public ownership. All this for the sake of those familiar bogies, inflation and the balance of payments, that frustrated the plans of the Labour Government of 1964–70 and which the Party had vowed not to accept as an excuse ever again. The bitter disputes within the Party which took place in 1967, 1968 and 1969 would seem like happy memories of the tranquil past. Return to Government is no recipe for an assured future for the Party.

THE ALTERNATIVE

One possibility that must be considered is that the role of the Labour Party as the main party of the Left may be taken over by the Liberal Party. Not since the last war have the Liberals had so much support as they have today. Their rivals have never been weaker. Liberals are untainted by the failure of post-war Governments; as one of their by-election victors, Clement Freud, observed, they 'had led a blameless life since 1916' (when they last formed a Liberal Government).*

When a party has been out of favour for more than a generation and suddenly revives, it would be unwise to assume that its new-found support is stably based. The disillusioned deserters from the Labour and Conservative camps, now searching for a new home, may be only temporary residents—'He that goeth about', said Bishop Hooker in his *Ecclesiastical Polity*, 'to

* *Observer*, July 29th, 1973.

persuade a multitude that they are not so well-governed as they ought to be, shall never want attentive and favourable readers, because they know the manifold defects where-unto every kind of regimen is subject; but the secret lets and difficulties, which in public proceedings are innumerable and inevitable, they have not ordinarily the judgement to consider.'

Certainly the Liberal style of fighting elections can attract a variety of dissenters. To begin with, 'community politics' has an obvious attraction for radicals. It has the same flavour as the pressure-group politics of movements like Shelter, which sprang up in the 'sixties and provided an outlet for radical energies which the conventional party framework did not provide. Community politics can appeal to anyone, from the Right as well as the Left, who welcomes the challenge to the establishment and feels that the system is not allowing people enough chance to have their say. One can be a Powellite, a Poujadiste or a Trotskyite, and support community politics. This is not to decry this form of participation, but to point out the difficulties that may arise when the Liberal Party comes to be considered by voters in a national role. It is not that the Liberals have no national policies, as their critics claim. They have lots of policies. The trouble is that most people do not know what they are, since Liberals normally capture headlines only when they win by-elections or win control of a local authority, as in 1973. Because they cannot form the next Government, and with such a small band of M.P.s cannot play a major part in the House of Commons, their policy statements are bound to attract less attention than Government White Papers or Labour's latest plan to nationalize ice-cream vendors.

It would be misleading to suggest that when Labour voters vote Labour, or Conservative voters vote Conservative, most of them know the detailed policies of their respective parties, or, for that matter, agree with these policies. But they probably have a clearer picture of the effect their votes will have than Liberal voters do at the present time. Many people still have only a vague notion who the Liberals are and what they stand for.

Three distinct elements are discernible in the Liberal Party.

The first is a remnant of the old Liberal tradition of Gladstone and Asquith, which was last a powerful element in the Party when Clement Davies was the Liberal leader. It is the most conservative element of the Party, with a strong streak of *laissez-faire*, and it exists mainly among the middle-aged. Next, there is a movement, prominent among the Young Liberals, which is sceptical about the possibility of reform through legislation and parliamentary debate, and which prefers direct action. In this, its approach is not unlike that of Trotskyites who reject 'the system'. It was this group which launched community politics as a method of campaigning. Lastly, there is the establishment of the Liberal Party, naturally most prominent at Westminster, which is responsible and radical in approach on the whole, and which would not find many points of difference from the Jenkinsites in the Labour Party.

In my view, there are two major obstacles in the path of the Liberal march to power. The first is that, as their policies become more widely known they will lose some of their support from the Right. Secondly, the drift to the Liberals from social democratic supporters of the Labour Party is likely, except in by-elections, to be a gradual process.

Tradition, loyalty and inertia are still immensely strong in politics, and because of this many social democrats will continue to feel that, warts and all, the Labour Party remains the best vehicle for radical change. Some radicals in the Labour Party, who reject the left-wing dogmatism that is now predominant, nevertheless want the Government to play a greater role in shaping the development of the economy and in ensuring the redistribution of income than is advocated by the Liberal Party. Many intellectuals will cling to the Labour Party so long as most of the academic brain-power that is anti-Conservative is still attached to it. However unhappy they may be with the control of the T.U.C. by the left wing, no major or middle-sized union is likely to abandon the Labour Party and transfer its support to the Liberals.

The very presence of the Jenkinsite group within the Labour Party will continue to attract support from social democrats who reject the Tribune brand of socialism. If the Liberals replace the Labour Party only gradually, the change-over could take a generation. Meanwhile, the Conservatives would have the lion's share of the power.

Suppose, however, that the Labour Party splits up. Suppose that the majority, or even at first a minority, of the social democratic group in Parliament grow weary of the long struggle to make a coalition of incompatibles work. Suppose that they recognize that they have no chance in the Party of playing a role more effective than that of a fig leaf of respectability, and that they pack up their bags and go. Politics in Britain would be transformed overnight. What might then start as a Lib–Lab alliance would soon emerge as a new radical or social democratic party.

Such a party would have great electoral appeal. When, in September 1972, *The Times* commissioned an opinion poll to investigate popular reaction to such a realignment, the poll revealed that it would be supported by a larger proportion of people than would vote either Tory or Labour. There would be 'twelve million Jenkinsites'. While the results of the by-elections of 1973 do not unequivocally confirm this poll, they are wholly consistent with it. Public reaction to my own by-election victory, in the form of about two thousand letters of congratulation and support (and a dozen of condemnation and disgust), strengthened the view—which I first formed early in 1972—that a social democratic party was not only desirable but feasible.

In the first place, it would attract the bulk of Labour votes. Labour has never held power as long or as often as might otherwise have been expected, because much of its natural support has been repelled, I believe, by the influence of its left wing (even when this influence was a minority one), and by the degree of control over the Party exercised by the trade unions. The cause of conscience, social justice and reform (the creed of Hugh Gaitskell) has a far larger constituency than the traditional socialism of the Tribune Group. It has been a constant theme of this book that all the evidence indicates that the left wing is supported only by a small minority in the country. If social democrats split off from the Labour Party, as they did in Lincoln, so that the left wing of the Party lies naked and exposed, as happened in Lincoln, most Labour voters would refuse to vote Labour.

A social democratic party, whatever its name, would attract most of the traditional Liberal vote, a vote of substantial proportions. It might also win over many people of progressive views who now vote Conservative but with reluctance, people who feel a need to choose between the major parties but who reject the Labour Party and turn to the Tories by default.

People will say that, alas, such a party cannot win power because it will have no funds. The financial support of the unions, it is felt, will save the Labour Party in the end, because other than the support of business, which goes to the Conservatives, it provides the only source of large-scale finance.

I leave to one side the need to reform British politics by financing parties of more than a minimum size from state funds, as many Continental countries do. If that were done, the dangers of parties or Governments being unduly influenced by pressure groups would be diminished. Even without such a reform, however, it should be possible to raise sufficient funds from individuals. The Democrats in the United States raise many times the sums which would be needed in Britain. One organization, Shelter, has managed to raise over a million pounds a year. Before the by-election in Lincoln, unsolicited gifts of money flowed into the headquarters of the Democratic Labour Association in sufficient quantities to finance an Agent and a full-time secretary; and contributions from individuals have since enabled me to set up with a modest staff a national pressure group for social democracy called the Campaign for Social Democracy. Funds on this scale multiplied proportionately for a major national party would support an effective organization.

In any event, it is not inconceivable that the defection of politicians from the Labour Party would be followed by the desertion of some important trade unions as well. A considerable number of trade union leaders, who are in the minority in the T.U.C., are sympathetic to the social democratic cause. However, it would clearly be a mistake for a new party to tie itself constitutionally to any unions which supported it. Financial support must be kept separate from voting power. Although moderate union leaders might be able to tolerate in practice the incomes policy to which a new party would almost certainly be committed, even they would be unlikely to be able to accept it in principle. Political co-operation does not require a common political identity.

A new party of this kind would be internationalist in its approach to Europe and the Third World, radical in its pursuit of social justice at home. It would promote industrial democracy and partnership in industry, redistribution of wealth—especially a redistribution of the wealth which is accrued through the accident of birth—and a redistribution of power away from the centre. It would see the necessity for transferring certain powers to Brussels, as outlined in Chapter 8. There is no reason why at the same time there should not be a transfer of other powers to Cardiff and Edinburgh, Exeter or Leeds.

Finally, as such a party would not consist of a coalition of people with a conflicting philosophy, it could discard the strict party discipline which stifles independent thought and action in the two main parties today. It could give Parliament a new lease of life.

No one can forecast with confidence that the Labour Party will split, and it is extremely unlikely to happen just before a General Election. A political divorce at any time can be as emotionally upsetting as a matrimonial one. M.P.s would find it difficult to abandon loyal supporters in their constituencies who had helped them in many elections in the past, or to abandon colleagues whose ideals were the same but who would feel unable to leave the Party. A split will come only when it is forced, when some M.P.s are compelled to realize that their continuation within the Party leaves them without public support or personal influence. M.P.s will take the fateful step only when they see that the decline of the Labour Party as one of the two major parties in politics is irreversible.

Those who leave the Labour Party will be called traitors to the cause. But there is no treason to parties. The only betrayal is of ideals, and there is no worse betrayal in politics.

APPENDIX A

APPEAL BY DICK TAVERNE

To the National Executive Committee Against the Decision of the General Management Committee of the Lincoln Party on June 19th, 1972

A. THE FACTS

I thought it might be convenient if I briefly set out the salient points of the history of this matter.

1. *Previous history*

Before the Common Market issue, there have been previous differences between myself and the present Chairman of the Party.

At my selection conference in January 1962, before the vote, the present Chairman and three of his colleagues (all of whom I believe were people now on the Executive Committee of the Lincoln Labour Party) walked out of the selection conference in protest against the views of all the candidates.

In April 1968, when I was Parliamentary Under-Secretary in the Home Office, the present Chairman asked the then Regional Organizer how they could get rid of their Member of Parliament, as they could not tolerate as their M.P. anyone who was a member of the Wilson Government.

2. *Recent events*

After I voted on October 28th in favour of entry into Europe, a motion of no confidence in the Member of Parliament was considered at the G.M.C. on November 16th. This was passed by 55 votes to 51, with 5 abstentions. At a further meeting of the

G.M.C. on December 6th, a recommendation of the Executive Committee was accepted that no further action be taken for the time being. A motion from the floor that the matter be dropped altogether was not carried after a tied vote of 45–45.

After this latter vote a meeting was arranged between myself and the officers to see if we could reconcile our differences. At this meeting the sole suggestion of the officers for a reconciliation was that I should voluntarily retire.

Subsequently, without my knowledge or that of the Management Committee as a whole, some fifty members of the Management Committee signed a petition to Transport House to which I can refer only in general terms as I have only learned of its contents indirectly. I believe it states that they recognized that I was and had been a good Member of Parliament for Lincoln; they accepted that I had given good service to the Labour Party; but they felt so strongly about my vote on the Common Market contrary to their wishes that they would like Transport House to find me another seat.

After the abortive meeting with the officers a further suggestion was made, which I welcomed, that the officers and myself might meet together with the National Agent. However, in April of this year the officers made it clear that they saw no purpose in such a meeting.

The future of the Member of Parliament was raised again after my resignation as a Shadow spokesman on April 11th. A meeting of the General Management Committee on May 15th decided by a vote of 55–38 to hold a special meeting on June 19th to consider a motion that the Member of Parliament should retire. On June 19th this motion was considered and passed by 75 votes to 50.

3. *Consultation*

It is, I suggest, of some importance that the majority of ordinary members of the party were given no opportunity to express their views on the issue of my resignation before the final meeting of the G.M.C.

The procedure adopted in 1970 at Party Conference requires

at least four weeks' notice before the final G.M.C. meeting. This, I suggest, was provided for to enable the wards and other constituent bodies affiliated to the party to meet and through them to give an opportunity to Party members to have their say. I assume that four weeks was the period provided because wards and others meet monthly.

In at least one case, Carholme Ward, despite requests from the Chairman (one of my supporters), the Secretary (one of my opponents) refused to hold a meeting at all.

In most cases, certainly in most wards, ordinary Party members did not receive notices of time or place of ward meetings during this period.

I know of no case where those who did get a notice of a ward meeting received an agenda that included the issue of the retirement of the Member of Parliament.

In the case of one ward (Minster Ward) members tried to raise the issue. The Chairman (a Vice-Chairman of the Party and one of my opponents) at first tried to prevent the matter from being discussed. When members insisted, he refused to divulge the terms of the motion to be considered by the G.M.C. and refused to allow a vote.

I know of only seven constituent branches of the Party where a vote was taken. In one ward the vote was against me. In six trade union branches (the A.S.W., the E.T.U., the General and Municipal, A.U.E.W. Number 6 branch, U.P.W. and P.O.E.W.) a vote was taken which was in my favour in each case.

The failure to give most members of the Party a chance to express their views was all the more serious in that all the evidence suggests strong support for me and strong opposition to the action of the G.M.C. amongst the public in Lincoln and amongst Labour supporters.

A poll commissioned by me and carried out by Mr Richard Jay of the Department of Government, University of Essex, showed that 71·3 per cent thought I was right to vote the way I did, 21·1 per cent thought I was wrong and 7·6 per cent did not know. On the question whether they approved or disapproved of me as their M.P., 79·2 per cent approved, 12·5 per cent disapproved and 8·3 per cent did not know. This poll was based on 607 replies to a postal inquiry. Full details have been sent to the Regional Organizer by Mr Jay.

A poll commissioned by the *Lincolnshire Chronicle*, a weekly paper, without my knowledge, concentrated on mainly Labour areas. They asked which way people voted and whether the decision of the G.M.C. to ask for my retirement was right. Of the 812 Labour voters asked, 17 per cent thought the G.M.C. was right and 76 per cent thought it was wrong. Full details of this poll have, I believe, been supplied to the National Agent.

These polls confirm the clear impression of the local daily paper (the *Lincolnshire Echo*), as well as the weekly paper, of my own widespread experience in Lincoln, as well as my postbag, and of the reports from my supporters.

B. GROUNDS OF APPEAL

1. *Procedural*

I appeal against the decision of the G.M.C. on the grounds that the procedure envisaged by the rules adopted at the 1970 Conference was not followed and that the decision was undemocratic.

As already stated, it seems to me obvious that the reason that two meetings are required with at least four weeks' interval is to consult the wards, etc. Why provide for two meetings? Why for four weeks' notice? One would have expected the officers and the agent to have ensured the widest possible consultation on a matter of this importance and to have seen to it that notice went to every member of the Party to attend his ward meeting with the future of the M.P. as one of the items on the agenda. This did not happen.

It may be argued that at a selection conference the affiliated bodies are not consulted. This is not a parallel. The list of candidates up for selection is probably not well known to the ordinary Party member. Selection requires listening to the speech of the candidates and testing them by question. When the future of an existing Member of Parliament is at stake, the position is quite different. The M.P. is known, or should be known, to the ordinary members of the Party. They all know his views, his political record and the way in which he has represented them at Westminster. All Party members have a direct interest in his future.

I urge therefore that the decision should not be allowed to stand because it was not democratically arrived at and all the signs point towards its being contrary to the wishes of the ordinary members of the Party.

2. *Substance*

(*a*) The decision of the Lincoln Labour Party G.M.C. denies the right to dissent which has been part of the proud history of the Labour Party. This is a right that has been recognized, not only for pacifists, but on all great issues of conscience and principle and deeply held conviction. Keir Hardie wrote in 1910:

> Where a member has a conscientious or other valid objection to supporting a finding of the Party, the almost invariable rule has been to allow him freedom of action, both of speech and vote, and this freedom has been frequently claimed and exerciseds.

At my selection conference in 1962 I specifically argued for entry into the Common Market as part of my belief in international socialism. In the by-election of 1962 and the General Elections of 1964, 1966 and 1970, I publicly stated my strong support for entry into the Common Market. There was no objection or criticism of these public declarations by my local Party at any time.

The Common Market is the only major issue on which I have differed from Party policy and on which I have not supported the Party by my vote.

When the moves against me were first made they were based entirely on my Market vote. It was repeatedly stated by the Chairman and other critics in the press and at G.M.C. meetings that they had no complaints about my record as a Member of Parliament.

(*b*) If the decision of the Lincoln Labour Party G.M.C. is allowed to stand, it will establish that Members of Parliament are delegates and not representatives, who have to accept instructions on particular votes. This is contrary to the views of the duties of M.P.s consistently upheld by the Party's leaders in Parliament throughout its parliamentary history.

I fully accept that I am accountable to local Party members as a whole for my general conduct as Member of Parliament. It would, however, I suggest, be wrong to allow a local Party to dismiss its Member because of one single vote.

(*c*) It is widely argued by my supporters, I suggest on solid ground, that to uphold the decision of the Management Committee would endanger the seat for Labour. I accept that in normal circumstances no Member of Parliament can be regarded as indispensable, especially if the majority is such that the seat is not very marginal. However, in this case the circumstances of my retirement would create an unusual situation. The polls already referred to suggest that ordinary voters disagree with the decision of the Management Committee. The basis of this feeling, I suggest, is not so much my general contribution to the constituency, although I hope this has been helpful, as the strong public feeling that a Member of Parliament should not be compelled to abandon his public commitments.

It might be felt that the N.E.C. has no right to interfere if procedure has been complied with. I maintain that it has not. If, however, the view of the N.E.C. is that there were no errors of procedure, I suggest that the whole reason for providing a specific right of appeal to a Member of Parliament in 1970 was to give him rights that go beyond procedure. Before 1970 the N.E.C. was always empowered to interfere if there had been irregularities. It made no new power to do so. The new power was presumably introduced to widen the powers of the N.E.C. It contains no reference to procedure. I therefore suggest that the obvious inference is that the N.E.C. is not restricted to considering procedural matters.

C. ACTION BY THE N.E.C.

1. I would ask the N.E.C. to allow me a personal hearing to elaborate the points made in this document and produce evidence on any disputed questions of fact.

2. I would welcome an inquiry by the N.E.C. into the whole background circumstances of the vote on June 19th. In particular I hope that they will look into the denial to ordinary members of the Party of a chance to express their views on a matter of such importance. I would also welcome an inquiry into the role of the Agent.

3. I would suggest that in the circumstances much the best solution would be an independently conducted poll of all Party members. To reconstitute the procedure laid down at Party Conference would be likely to deepen wounds that should be healed. I would myself accept the verdict of this poll and agree that I cannot be the Party's candidate if I have lost the support of the majority of its members. At the same time it would seem reasonable to expect the officers of the Party to accept the verdict of such a poll if it is favourable to me.

4. I would welcome any assistance the N.E.C. could give in seeking a reconciliation in the Lincoln constituency between the two groups of active members who are deeply divided.

(signed) DICK TAVERNE

APPENDIX B

CAMPAIGN FOR SOCIAL DEMOCRACY: A STATEMENT OF AIMS—REALISM—SOCIAL JUSTICE—DEMOCRACY

The Campaign for Social Democracy aims to change the course of British politics. It claims no instant solutions, nor will it make promises that are impossible to fulfil. It will attempt to spell out not only the benefits of its policies, but also the sacrifices. The underlying principles of the campaign are that policies shall be realistic, that they shall be designed to promote the cause of social justice, and that they shall be pursued through democratic means.

Realism

Today the stale political battle between the extremes of old-fashioned 'free enterprise' and class-oriented 'socialism' has no more relevance than the Civil War between the Cavaliers and Roundheads. In place of dogma, the campaign is based on a philosophy of social responsibility combined with maximum personal freedom. The starting point is realism. There are no panaceas, and today's solutions may be inappropriate tomorrow. No one party or group has a monopoly of wisdom, and only those willing to admit mistakes can learn from them.

Social justice

The Campaign for Social Democracy is a campaign for a society of equal opportunities and equal rights: a society in which the quality of people's lives is not determined by class, sex, race or the privilege of inherited wealth; a society in which the successful give help to the deprived, the healthy to the infirm and the young to the old. Social justice is not only right in itself—it is the only basis on which a complex modern society can function without destructive conflict.

Democracy

Democracy is the basis of our way of life. No cause, however just it appears, no conviction, however sincerely held, should be pursued by means which endanger the rule of law. Reform must come through persuasion by elected representatives, not coercion by militant minorities. When politicians make promises they cannot fulfil; when parties in opposition reject policies they pursued in power, and espouse in power policies they denounced in opposition; disillusionment and apathy follow.

These principles command wide assent. It is easy to agree to the ends; the test comes in determining the means. As it progresses, the campaign will put forward constructive proposals on the most important national issues; the following guidelines indicate its general stance.

The Distribution of Incomes and Wealth

A prices and incomes policy should not be a temporary expedient, born of panic and abandoned when an election looms. Without it, there is no way of achieving greater fairness in the rewards for work, or of fighting inflation without large-scale unemployment. Unrestrained collective bargaining rewards the strong, the militant and those with scarce skills at the expense of the weak—those who live on fixed incomes and those whose dedication makes them reluctant to strike. For such a policy to work it must be comprehensive and fair, and must have statutory framework. It must be accompanied by measures redistributing private wealth and maintaining a high level of public spending on schools, hospitals, pensions and relieving regional disparities, but not on profligate prestige projects.

In practical terms this means the acceptance of a permanent and independent body to monitor key prices and wages; it means that taxation should be more, not less, progressive; that an accessions tax on the recipients of wealth should replace estate duty.

Social Democracy at Work

Britain is respected the world over for its democratic institutions. But, on the shop floor and in the office, Britain is often less democratic than many other European countries.

Industry cannot thrive on a 'them and us' conflict between management and labour. People must be given more say in decisions that affect their working lives. Secret decisions in the board-room, affecting the welfare of thousands of employees and of many local communities, are not the best way of ensuring that the public interest is served. Commerce, industry and Government must disclose more information and must consult those affected by their decisions. Company Law and Industrial Law must provide effective sanctions against the abuse of power, whether by business corporations, financiers or trade unions.

Government and Industry

The Campaign for Social Democracy seeks wider social accountability for industry but opposes wholesale nationalization. It accepts the mixed economy and believes that Public Ownership is only one of many ways to promote social and economic objectives wider than the maximization of profit. It is crucial that government intervention should stem from a consistent philosophy, not from arbitrary decisions or from skilful lobbying of sectional groups. Taxpayers' money should not be used to rescue shareholders from the consequences of inefficient management.

To channel investment funds where they are needed, there should be an independent body insulated from the day-to-day pressures of political expediency, and operating on clear and pre-defined guidelines approved by Parliament. To a large extent, social responsibility in industry can be achieved by fuller disclosure and fiscal means.

Economic Growth and the Environment

The destruction of our cities and of our countryside affects us all. Further, the wasteful exploitation of our national resources may prejudice the well-being of our children and grandchildren. We must not deface our country with motorways, airports, office blocks and quarries unless we are quite sure they serve a more valuable purpose than the houses, amenities and agricultural land they destroy.

What is required is a balanced strategy for economic development which weighs the benefits of producing more wealth against the possible adverse side-effects and against the depletion of finite resources. Technology which preserves resources and enhances the environment should be encouraged. Cars, refrigerators and washing machines must be built to last, and not to fall apart, and more waste products should be recycled. Above all, society must value the provision of services and amenities to people more than the limitless production of goods.

Britain and Europe

The Campaign for Social Democracy supports Britain's membership of the European Community. Problems concerning the environment, the needs of the regions and the control of multinational companies are matters for solution at international level. By active and committed participation in the work of the Community Britain can help to make it an instrument for achieving social democratic aims.

First, the financial obligations of the Common Agricultural Policy—which must itself be modified—should be matched by benefits from the Community's Regional and Social Funds. Secondly, Europe's obligation to developing countries must be more clearly recognized. The campaign will press for more generous trading agreements, particularly with those Commonwealth countries to whom Britain owes a special responsibility. Thirdly, it will work for greater political unity and more democratic control within the Community. The European Parliament should have more power and should be directly elected.

Support the Campaign

Courage, idealism and fresh thinking are badly needed in British politics today. Voters in every part of the country have shown in by-elections and local government elections that they are weary of the timidity, dogma and cynicism of the party machines. Ordinary people *can* influence events.

This campaign aims to give expression to their feelings and aspirations and to harness them in the cause of reform.